The Way of Suffering

READINGS FOR AN ENLIGHTENED LIFE

The Way of Suffering

READINGS FOR AN ENLIGHTENED LIFE

Michael Leach, James T. Keane,
Doris Goodnough, editors

ORBIS BOOKS
Maryknoll, New York 10545

Founded in 1970, Orbis Books endeavors to publish works that enlighten the mind, nourish the spirit, and challenge the conscience. The publishing arm of the Maryknoll Fathers and Brothers, Orbis seeks to explore the global dimensions of the Christian faith and mission, to invite dialogue with diverse cultures and religious traditions, and to serve the cause of reconciliation and peace. The books published reflect the views of their authors and do not represent the official position of the Maryknoll Society. To learn more about Maryknoll and Orbis Books, please visit our website at www.maryknollsociety.org.

Library of Congress Cataloging-in-Publication Data

Names: Leach, Michael, editor. | Keane, James Thomas, editor. | Goodnough, Doris, editor.

Title: The way of suffering : readings for an enlightened life / Michael Leach, James T. Keane, Doris Goodnough, editors.

Description: Maryknoll, New York : Orbis Books, 2020. | Series: The way series | Includes bibliographical references and index. | Summary: "A collection of inspiring stories, poems, and essays that show the path to growth, wisdom, and compassion that comes through suffering"— Provided by publisher.

Identifiers: LCCN 2019048014 | ISBN 9781626983601 (paperback)

Subjects: LCSH: Suffering—Religious aspects—Christianity.

Classification: LCC BV4909 .W39 2020 | DDC 248.8/6—dc23

LC record available at https://lccn.loc.gov/2019048014

Suffering is inevitable, but not necessary.

—THOMAS HORA, M.D.

Contents

Contents

THE WAY OF SUFFERING

Contents

Contents

THE WAY OF SUFFERING

Sparks
JOHN DONNE, 1 CORINTHIANS 12:26,
THOMAS MERTON
page 139

Contents

Contents

Introduction

You scream,
I scream,
We all scream
For ice cream.

Anything to find relief from "the slings and arrows of outrageous fortune." Ben & Jerry's Cherry Garcia or Peanut Butter Chocolate from Häagen-Dazs. It doesn't matter. We'll do anything to escape suffering. Medicine, money, sex, power, fame, or even ice cream to dull the ache of anxiety. It doesn't matter. Nothing works for long.

We live in a dualistic world of good and bad, pleasure and pain, darkness and light. We can't have one side of the coin without the other. One will follow the other as surely as a black and white horror film follows a technicolor fairy tale at this crazy drive-in movie theater we call the world. We all scream many times in life, not for ice cream but for an end to our bouts of suffering.

Buddha observed that suffering in this world is inevitable, the natural result of our insatiable desires, our wanting this and not wanting that, our not getting what we want or getting what we want. The enlightened response to suffering, said Buddha, was compassion and loving kindness, to ourselves as well as others. Jesus showered compassion on all who suffered, and raised the dead and healed the sick and above all showed us all that we, like him, could transcend sufferings. "In this world you shall have trials and tribulations but be of good cheer, for I have overcome the world" (John 16:33). Jesus went on to emphasize that whatever he did we could do also (John 14:12).

To overcome the world is to rise above it with our feet on the ground, to realize that, in truth, "we live and move and have our being in God" (Acts 17:28). God is not a magic man in a place in the sky but the always-everywhere-active, unconditional Love in which "there is no change or shifting shadow" (James 1:17). The remedies of this world are counterfeit. Only "perfect love can cast out fear" (1 John 4:18). And that love is nearer to us than hands and feet. It is the ground of our being.

The stories, essays, and poems in this book are not quick fixes or elixirs. They acknowledge the experience of our sufferings, unsparingly. Taken as a whole they are like fingers pointing in the direction of the moon. The fingers are not the moon and these chapters are not God, but together they form a compass needle that can guide us to enlightenment, a spiritual understanding of God and our relationship to God and all beings that grounds healings.

Dr. Thomas Hora, a psychiatrist whose practice was infused with spiritual teachings, counseled that there are only two ways to become enlightened, through wisdom or through suffering, and that for most of us it is suffering that motivates us to turn away from the things of the world for relief, and to turn to God for healing. "We fix our eyes not on what is seen, but on what is unseen, since what is seen is temporary, but what is unseen lasts forever" (2 Corinthians 4:18). To see with the eyes of the soul is to choose Love and glimpse the face of God.

The Way of Suffering is the fourth in a series of writings on values that transform us. First was *The Way of Gratitude*. Then *The Way of Kindness*, followed by *The Way of Forgiveness*. Like the Star Wars movies where the first one (*A New Hope*) was really the fourth, and the fourth (*The Phantom Menace*) was really the first, *The Way of Suffering* might best be first to read because it begins at the beginning, with our broken world. As poet Leonard Cohen sang, "There is a crack in everything. That's how the light gets in."

Nobody said enlightenment is easy.

But it happens to all of us, if only for brief moments, moments we always remember, that reassure us everything is all right, and that see us through till the next time our whole being screams out to God for another miracle. It has happened to you before. *The Way of Suffering* and its companion volumes say be patient and choose love, forgiveness, gratitude, and kindness. Miracles will happen again.

Michael Leach,
James T. Keane,
Doris Goodnough

PART ONE

NO EASY ANSWERS

Keep knocking and the door will be opened to you.

🌿

A Beginning

Therese J. Borchard

I had suffered a nervous breakdown. The suffering was unbearable. My husband rushed me to Johns Hopkins Hospital.

Fear consumed me.

Until I saw Jesus.

In the lobby was a ten-and-a-half foot tall marble statue of Jesus, his arms extended toward those in desperate need of healing. The inscription, written in capital letters on the pedestal, read: "Come unto me all ye that are weary and heavy laden, and I will give you rest."

I stood in front of Jesus for a while, tempted to touch his robe like the hemorrhaging woman who got her miracle in the gospels of Mark and Luke. She had bled for twelve years, "had endured much under many physicians, and had spent all that she had; and she was no better" (Mark 5:26). Just by touching the hem of Jesus' cloak, this ailing woman was healed of her disease, because her faith was so great.

"I believe, Jesus," I said to the statue, imagining myself touching the hem of Jesus' real robe, "I believe."

And I wept at his feet.

Why Is There Suffering?

James Martin, SJ

Horrifying disasters around the world unfold before our eyes on television and online, not only wrenching the hearts of every compassionate person, but also raising for the believer an age-old question: Why do we suffer?

That immense question, or the "problem of evil," has bedeviled theologians, saints, mystics—all believers—for thousands of years. The question can also be framed as: How could a good God allow suffering?

First, we have to admit that none of the answers to "Why do we suffer?" can completely satisfy us when faced with real suffering—our own or that of others. The best answer to "Why do we suffer?" may be "We don't know." Anyone who offers you "the answer" is either a liar or a fool. And has probably never faced real suffering.

Second, we have to admit that belief in God may mean belief in a God whose ways will always remain mysterious. In an article in *America* magazine, Rabbi Daniel Polish, author of *Talking about God*, put it succinctly. "I do not believe in a God whose will or motives are crystal clear to me. And as a person of faith, I find myself deeply suspicious of those who claim such insight."

Polish goes on to quote Rabbi Abraham Joshua Heschel, "To the pious man knowledge of God is not a thought within his grasp . . ." This is the greatest challenge of faith, says Polish, "to live with a God we cannot fully understand, whose actions we explain at our own peril."

But while there are no definitive answers to the question of suffering, and while we may never fully understand it, there are what you might call "perspectives" offered by the Jewish and Christian traditions.

Perhaps the most helpful was the belief that God can accompany us in our suffering. And that it was okay, and even healthy, to lament these things before God, as many of the psalms do. That it was "mysterious," something I might never understand, like Job's question in the Old Testament, but that I could still continue to be in relationship with God. That I could try (but would sometimes fail) to emulate the patient way that Jesus faced suffering. That Jesus, who had suffered intensely in his life, could be, through my relationship in prayer with him, someone who understood my trials, small though they may be, and who could accompany me in them.

Most of all, that God could somehow be with me through times of pain, and small signs of hope could become apparent when I accepted the reality of suffering. In vulnerability, in poverty of spirit, in brokenness, we are often able to meet God in new and unexpected ways.

Perhaps this is because we are more open to God's presence: when our defenses are down, when we have nothing left, we are more open. This is why people who suffer are sometimes seen as becoming more religious or spiritual. They are not becoming more irrational, but more open.

This is not the "why" of suffering, nor does it "explain" suffering; but it can sometimes be part of the overall experience.

But my suffering is small. When I worked in East Africa as a young Jesuit, I met refugees who had seen their brothers and sisters murdered before their eyes. Also during my Jesuit training, I knew a woman in Boston who had been confined to a hospital bed for over 20 years. And recently a close friend's young wife was suddenly diagnosed with a brain tumor, and, after returning from the hospital, when I wept at home for the two of them, I saw in an instant how little I had ever suffered compared to them, and to others. My suffering is very small.

Moreover, my suffering is not yours. Nor are my own perspectives on suffering meant to be yours. Just as every believer must find a personal path to God, so must he or she find personal perspective on suffering. And while the collective wisdom of the community is a great resource, the platitudes and bromides offered by otherwise well-meaning believers as quick-fix answers are often unhelpful.

Sometimes those easy answers short-circuit the process of deeper individual reflection.

Believers are rightly suspicious of easy answers to suffering. My mother once told me of an elderly nun who was living at a retirement home with my 90-year-old grand-mother. One day the woman's religious superior came to visit. The elderly nun began to speak about how much pain she was enduring. "Think of Jesus on the Cross," said her superior.

The elderly nun replied, "Jesus was only on the Cross for three hours." Easy answers usually do more harm than good.

Richard Leonard, an Australian Jesuit priest, wrote about his experience with such facile answers in his book, *Where the Hell Is God?*

Richard's family has been touched with great suffering. His father died of a massive stroke at the age of 36, leaving his mother to care for Richard, then two, and his siblings. At dawn on Richard's 25th birthday, his Jesuit superior woke him to summon him to the phone for an urgent call from his mother. His sister Tracey, a nurse working at a healthcare facility for aboriginal people, had been involved in a terrible car accident. When Richard and his mother reached the hospital their worst fears were confirmed: Tracey was a quadriplegic.

Through tears, Richard's mother began to ask him questions about suffering that put his faith to the test. Richard called it "the most painful and important theological discussion I will ever have in my life." "Where the hell is God?" his mother asked.

Richard's answer to his mother was, in essence, that God was with them in their suffering. "I think God is devastated," said Richard. "Like the God who groans with loss in Isaiah, and like Jesus who weeps at his best friend's tomb, God was not standing outside our pain, but was a companion within it, holding us in his arms, sharing our grief and pain."

Besides the idea that suffering can sometimes open us up to new ways of experiencing God, this is the theological insight that I find most helpful in times of pain: the image of the God who has suffered, the God who shares our grief, the God who understands. Much in the same way that you instinctively turn to a friend who has already gone through the same trial you are facing, you can more easily turn to Jesus in prayer, who suffered. "For we do not have a high priest who is unable to sympathize with our weaknesses," as St. Paul's the Letter to the Hebrews says.

Richard takes a dim view of those who offer glib answers in the face of suffering. "Some of the most appalling and frightening letters," he writes, came from "some of the best Christians I knew." Tracey must have done something to offend God, some said. Others suggested that her suffering was a "glorious building block . . . for her mansion [in heaven] when she dies." Others wrote that his family is truly "blessed," because "God only sends crosses to those who can bear them." Or, more simply, that it is all a "mystery" that simply needed to be accepted, almost unthinkingly.

My friend rejected these answers in favor of a hard look at the reality of suffering, one that only comes with the long struggle to have an "intelligent discussion about the complexities of where and how the Divine presence fits into our fragile and human world."

When we are suffering, our friends will want to help us make sense of our pain, and they will often offer answers like the ones Richard described. Some answers may work for us. Others may leave us cold or even be offensive.

But, in the end, every believer must come to grapple with suffering for ourselves. And while our religious traditions also provide us with important resources, ultimately, we must find an approach that enables us to confront pain and loss honestly with God.

Suffering is indeed a "mystery" for most believers, but it is not something that we should ignore, but one that we should engage with all our mind, heart and soul.

🌿

3

I Don't Have an Explanation, and Yet . . .

Maryanne J. Kane

My biggest regret? Never finding an answer to the big question.

If God really is our Abba-Father, our "loving Daddy," how can God allow his children to starve, to be abused, to suffer from terminal illnesses? Who hasn't asked this big question: "Why does God permit pain and suffering when God could easily end pain and suffering?"

Theological explanations include the concept of original sin, Jesus dying on the cross for our sins and free will. And yet these theological theories bring no peace while reading a newspaper filled with war, cruelty, desolation. My devout Catholic mother confidently advises prayer and reflection as a means of clarity. It took me a long time to realize what that means.

About 40 years ago, I remember praying, pleading, begging, tearfully imploring God for a miracle.

I had joined fellow high school graduates for the traditional senior week at the Jersey Shore—what's not to love about that?

Day one, I lay 12 hours on the hot, burning sand and returned to the hotel feeling sick. The next morning, I woke up bloated, blistered, nauseous, and weak. Friends administered cold creams, moisturizers, baby oil, even Vaseline on the burns. Unfortunately, the sharing from various jars infected the open blisters.

In about two months, my face exploded with six to seven large red welts—just in time for freshman year at college. Our family doctor recommended slicing into the sores to relieve the ever-swelling facial pus-bags. I asked him, "Won't that leave scars all over my face?"

"Yes," he said.

As I rushed out of the office, sobbing, Mom promised me, "We'll get this fixed." Sure enough, she did her research and found a well-regarded dermatologist at a teaching hospital. The following four years, every Saturday, week after week, Mom and I would visit the dermatologist's. Painful facial injections of Retin-A were applied to the huge, discolored open sores. Yes, it's as disgusting as it sounds.

Fortunately, I attended a private women's Catholic college. The small environment, daily visits to chapel and a spiritual director provided comfort. I embraced the spiritual foundation program, enmeshed in continual prayer: prayers of petition ("Please, fix my face!"), prayers of bargaining ("If you fix my face, I'll spend the rest of my life doing good works!"), prayers of pity ("God, you are not listening to me.")

I spent my college years in the library completing work-study hours and at weekly dermatologist visits. Summers between semesters were spent working as a file clerk in center city. Every morning, I joined the working world on the 13 trolley. The trolley ride was pleasant enough, but the continual oozing, pus-filled facial sores made passengers stare. Understandably, people were concerned about the spread of infection. I had to hold tissues to my face when the sores seeped guck.

Many, many, many mornings, when the sores were especially active, I just wanted to hide in my room. Mom's advice: "This is a life choice you need to make. It won't be the first difficult experience for you. You can sit in your room, mope, be unproductive, or you can get over yourself, go to work and make a salary for your college tuition. Pray to God for strength to endure this cross."

Best. Advice. Ever. Pity wouldn't do any good. I didn't stay home. I sucked it up—and continued to pray for a miracle. The cliché "Time heals all wounds" had truth. In about four years, the abrasions healed and faded, just in time for job interviews.

But now, when I look back on the quality of my prayer, I am embarrassed. Then I remind myself that I was young. A 20-year-old's depth of prayer for a miracle, while self-serving and myopic, is still a testament of belief in God. My biggest mistake confused spirituality and religion. One can be religious without an ounce of spirituality. No matter how many rosaries I recited, my sores weren't going to magically dissolve in an instant.

One can also be spiritual without much religion. Eventually, I came to see my experience with the eye of my soul. I began to realize that the suffering I felt with a facial disfigurement was nurturing in me a sincere empathy toward others in pain—greater or lesser, it made no difference.

"Why does a loving God permit pain?" I can honestly say, for the life of me, I don't know. But I sincerely thank God for answering my prayers in an unexpected way 40 years ago. Maybe in 1978, I couldn't see the wisdom of a loving God providing me with a wise mom's advice to get over myself. Surely in 1978, God gifted me with the grace to transcend a painful experience and evolve into a more compassionate person. My pain, upon reflection, became my biggest opportunity for growth.

No, I don't have a big answer to the big question. I can give testament, however, that what seemed like endless pain at the time was really an eternal blessing.

4

🌿

Changing Our Relationship to Pain

Victor M. Parachin

Rather than give the body relief, give relief to the mind: when the mind is at peace, the body is not distressed.

—YAMADA MUMON

The following is a very well-known story, but is cited here because its deeper meaning is often missed. Kisa Gotami's daughter died, leaving her mother in agony over the loss. Kisa's grief felt unbearable and manifested itself in body and mind. Desperately seeking relief, she remembered that the Buddha was capable of miracles. So she approached the Buddha, pleading for her daughter to be brought back to life. The Buddha, filled with compassion for Kisa, promised he would help her, but on one condition: she needed to bring him some mustard seed from a home that had never experienced sorrow.

Filled with new hope, Kisa set off on a search. "This should not be difficult," she thought. She knew that mustard seed was a common spice found in almost every home in the village. However, as she knocked on door after door, she heard one sad story after another. Every time she asked, "Has there been suffering and sorrow in this home?" she heard a new tale of pain:

"Oh, yes, Grandfather died last year."

"Yes, my son was born with a clubfoot and is unable to walk."

"My mother is desperately ill and will soon die."

"I lost two daughters in childbirth and have just miscarried again."

"My husband, the father of our four children, was killed in an accident."

It was not long before Kisa realized that suffering was universal. No human being could escape loss and sorrow. Kisa reflected on her experience and on the Buddha's suggestion to find mustard seed from a home that had never experienced sorrow. Before long, she returned to the Buddha, becoming one of his earliest and most devoted followers.

The usual interpretation of this story is to say that Kisa's grief was eased simply because she discovered that others suffer as well. However, there is more to glean from that famous story. Simply knowing that other people experience loss was not enough to remove Kisa's grief. The loss of a child is, after all, one of life's harshest blows, and one from which some people never rebound. Obviously something happened to Kisa as a result of her search, and it was this: Her new perspective—that suffering is universal—changed her relationship to her pain. The pain was still there, but it was no longer the driving force of her thoughts and actions. She had been clinging tightly to the view that her child should not have died, that life dealt her an unfair blow, that she should have had the opportunity to see her daughter grow up, marry, have children, and so on. She victimized herself by wishing her world would be as it once was.

Somehow, the realization that suffering is found in all lives altered her perspective, changing her relationship with her pain. Although Kisa probably missed her daughter all of her life, the anguish and anger of the loss receded. By understanding deeply that suffering is universal, she was able to free herself from her pain and begin to experience hope and joy along with her loss and grief.

The lesson that the Buddha hoped Kisa would learn is one we need to absorb today whenever events come our way that we label "unfortunate" and "tragic." We will still suffer, but if we can hold off attaching more emotional turmoil to the issue, then we can be free of the pain our attachments create. This insight is also demonstrated in a more current setting in the following story.

A school system in a large city had a special program to help hospitalized children keep up with their schoolwork. One day, a teacher who worked in the program received a routine call asking her to visit such a child. She was given the child's name, hospital, and room number. Her instructions were to help the boy with lessons in grammar.

That same day, the teacher went to see the boy. No one had mentioned to her that the youth had been badly burned and was in great pain. Caught off guard by the boy's disfiguring burns, his bandaged face, and his obvious physical pain, she struggled through the lesson. When she left the hospital room, the teacher was disappointed with herself, feeling that she had not accomplished much with her hospitalized student.

However, upon returning the next day, a nurse asked her: "What did you do with that boy? Ever since you visited yesterday, his attitude toward recovery has improved." The teacher was quite surprised, and listened carefully as the nurse explained that the entire staff was worried about the youth. He had not been responding effectively to treatment, nor was he showing much improvement. "After your visit, he became more responsive to treatment. It's as though he's decided to live," the nurse explained. The explanation for the boy's remarkable transformation came two weeks later, when the boy quietly explained that he had completely given up hope until the teacher arrived. Everything changed when he came to a simple realization, which he expressed this way: "They wouldn't send a teacher to work with me on grammar if I was dying, would they?"

Elements of that story are worth examining closely. At the end of the story, the boy is still in physical pain. The sight of his burns is no less disturbing and frightening.

Bandages over his face continue to keep him in the dark. Yet, even in the darkness, he begins to experience the light of hope. This story makes this crucial point: It is the boy's relationship to his pain that has changed, and that has relieved him of feeling hopeless. Especially insightful is the nurse's statement about the boy: "It's as though he's decided to live." Her comment brings out the truth that the attitude we take toward our painful situations is a matter of choice. We can either lay more emotional baggage onto our traumas, or we can accept what has happened. Without the additional emotional baggage, we are free to deal with the matter in a rational, healthy, constructive, and balanced way.

Sparks

*Our whole life consists of despairing of
an answer and seeking an answer.*

—DOROTHEE SOELLE

*Let difficulty transform you. And it
will. In my experience, we just need
help in learning how not to run away.*

—PEMA CHÖDRÖN

*Suffering is grace, a gift given in order
to awaken you.*

—RAM DASS

❧

5

It's OK to Despair
and Swear at God

Michael Leach

Job did. Jesus did, too. Sooner or later, we all do.

Life pushes us to the brink and we're left hanging over the cliff with one hand grasping a clump of grass and looking down at the abyss. Despair clutches our throat and what's left of our heart cries out to a silent God. Our only comfort is the words of Butch Cassidy to the Sundance Kid: "Don't worry. The fall will kill you."

It happened to me last week. It had to do with my wife and Alzheimer's and poop—here, there and everywhere. I didn't like cleaning it up, and when Vickie expressed her frustration by again resisting my help, I blurted out, "What's the matter with you? I'm trying to help you!" And when the poop on her bare feet spread into other rooms like vandals, I yelled, "You're killing me!"

I wiped my hands on my pants, hugged Vickie, and said, "I'm sorry. You didn't deserve that." I knew my anger was awful and the weight of anguish made me woozy so I hugged her some more to squeeze the fear out of both of us.

After I bathed us both with a hand-held shower spray like circus elephants, I wrapped Vickie in her friendliest PJs, placed her in the embrace of the recliner in the family room, and turned on "Ellen" who was talking like an adult to Sophia Grace and Rosie. I went upstairs and closed the door of our bedroom. I tried to take three deep Andrew Weil breaths, in and out, in and out, but blew up on the second exhale. "God," I yelled, 'you're an __hole! An __hole! You know that?!" I *grrrrd* fiercely.

I suppose my scream was a projection of my own guilt, but so what, it got the poison out. And I knew it wasn't blasphemy because the god I swore at wasn't God. It wasn't the all-loving, all-active, everywhere, benevolent Wisdom I needed more than ever, but the god of my childhood who punishes us as part of his curriculum, who never gives us more pain than we can handle, who allows us to be eaten by lions so we can prove our faith, and who takes babies away from their mothers so they can be happier with him in heaven. That guy. He tries to kill us no matter how well we grow in wisdom, age, and grace. Interviewer James Lipton asked Robert DeNiro what he'd like to hear God say to him when he entered the pearly gates. Jimmy the Gent from "Goodfellas" scowled: "Him? He's got a lot to answer for."

A friend of mine, Vinita Hampton Wright, posted this on her Facebook the other day: "What I love about my life today: I did not awaken in despair, which seems to happen a lot lately. Got up, showered, prayed, walked the dog, took the train, bought a bagel and coffee, and now I'm sitting here at work, and I do not feel that everything is coming to an end. If you have never felt this way, try not to judge me, and be grateful that this is not part of your natural makeup."

What happened to Vickie happens to me, happens to Vinita, and happens to everyone in one form or another at one time or another. St. Augustine said, "God had one son on earth without sin, but never one without suffering." Vinita's friends commented:

"Vinita, I've been feeling that way all day today. Hopefully tomorrow will be better."

"Been there, feeling a bit that way today, so no judgment."

"For several months while living in San Francisco I felt like the whole world was conspiring against me: buildings, trees, people. It was a rough time in my life."

"Been there. Done that. We all have. Thanks for posting this."

"Thank you for articulating this, Vinita. I often wake up feeling such despair, and I too cherish the days that feel steady, hopeful, normal. I hope your work is rich and good today."

People will always be kind. That is good to know.

I have also found it good to know that a prayer of surrender to the real God—the love who knows what we need before we do—is the fastest antidote to despair. Its core is, "Thy will be done. Thine, not mine."

The truth is, God doesn't want to hurt us! His will for us is good, pleasing and perfect (Romans 12:2). "Thy will be done, not mine" is a powerful prayer of petition because it puts the control where it belongs, in the hands of omnipotent love. It is a prayer of humility that brings surprises. Just as the eye has not seen the beauty that God has in store for us in heaven, we can't imagine the ways our problems will be solved on earth or, most likely, simply dissolve in our prayer of surrender.

I can't tell you how many times I have screamed out in my car over the years about the pain that comes from what I want or don't want to happen, what I think should or shouldn't be: "God, I can't take this anymore. It's killing me. Take this problem away. I give it to you. I place it on the altar of your love. I can't figure it out or change it or make it go away. I don't want to think about it anymore. I give up. I give it all to you. *Your* will be done. Yours is way better for me than mine. I'm done, Lord. Finished. It's yours. *Yours.* Thank you."

I am learning it's not the poop but making judgments about it that drives us mad. Job found peace only when he stopped obsessing and comparing his life with others. He let go and let god be God. I sometimes try to escape my life by fantasizing a different one in which I am the star and can do whatever I want without consequences and nothing bad ever happens to me. That always brings me down. Poop happens. None of us gets out of this thing without trouble. Jesus cried to his Father from the cross: "My God, my God, why have you forsaken me?" But he forgave the thief and the soldiers with their spears and whips and his garments. He let it go. His last words: "Father, into your hands I commit my spirit. It is finished."

The prayer of surrender reconciles, brings rest: It stops us from shuffling guilt and fear and anger thoughts in our mind like a stacked deck of cards. Handing our worries over to the real God who doesn't play games brings closure, lets us get on with our life (till the next problem when we have to do it all over again), and now and then have a laugh at the folly of being human. There's no other way. Try it.

🍂

6

The Value
of Suffering

Pico Iyer

Hundreds of Syrians are apparently killed by chemical weapons, and the attempt to protect others from that fate threatens to kill many more. A child perishes with her mother in a tornado in Oklahoma, the month after an 8-year-old is slain by a bomb in Boston. Runaway trains claim dozens of lives in otherwise placid Canada and Spain. At least 46 people are killed in a string of coordinated bombings aimed at an ice cream shop, bus station and famous restaurant in Baghdad. Does the torrent of suffering ever abate—and can one possibly find any point in suffering?

Wise men in every tradition tell us that suffering brings clarity, illumination; for the Buddha, suffering is the first rule of life, and insofar as some of it arises from our own wrongheadedness—our cherishing of self—we have the cure for it within. Thus in certain cases, suffering may be

an effect, as well as a cause, of taking ourselves too seri-
ously. I once met a Zen-trained painter in Japan, in his
90s, who told me that suffering is a privilege, it moves us
toward thinking about essential things and shakes us out
of shortsighted complacency; when he was a boy, he said,
it was believed you should pay for suffering, it proves such
a hidden blessing.

Yet none of that begins to apply to a child gassed to
death (or born with AIDS or hit by a "limited strike").
Philosophy cannot cure a toothache, and the person who
starts going on about its long-term benefits may induce a
headache, too. Anyone who's been close to a loved one suffering from depression knows that the vicious cycle behind
her condition means that, by definition, she can't hear the
logic or reassurances we extend to her; if she could, she
wouldn't be suffering from depression.

Occasionally, it's true, I'll meet someone—call him
myself—who makes the same mistake again and again,
heedless of what friends and sense tell him, unable even
to listen to himself. Then he crashes his car, or suffers a
heart attack, and suddenly calamity works on him like an
alarm clock; by packing a punch that no gentler means
can summon, suffering breaks him open and moves him
to change his ways.

Occasionally, too, I'll see that suffering can be in the eye
of the beholder, our ignorant projection. The quadriplegic
asks you not to extend sympathy to her; she's happy, even
if her form of pain is more visible than yours. The man
on the street in Calcutta, India, or Port-au-Prince, Haiti,

overturns all our simple notions about the relation of terrible conditions to cheerfulness and energy and asks whether we haven't just brought our ideas of poverty with us.

But does that change all the many times when suffering leaves us with no seeming benefit at all, and only a resentment of those who tell us to look on the bright side and count our blessings and recall that time heals all wounds (when we know it doesn't)? None of us expects life to be easy; Job merely wants an explanation for his constant unease. To live, as Nietzsche (and Roberta Flack) had it, is to suffer; to survive is to make sense of the suffering.

That's why survival is never guaranteed.

OR put it as Kobayashi Issa, a haiku master in the 18th century, did: "This world of dew is a world of dew," he wrote in a short poem. "And yet, and yet. . . ." Known for his words of constant affirmation, Issa had seen his mother die when he was 2, his first son die, his father contract typhoid fever, his next son and a beloved daughter die.

He knew that suffering was a fact of life, he might have been saying in his short verse; he knew that impermanence is our home and loss the law of the world. But how could he not wish, when his 1-year-old daughter contracted smallpox, and expired, that it be otherwise?

After his poem of reluctant grief, Issa saw another son die and his own body paralyzed. His wife died, giving birth to another child, and that child died, maybe because of a careless nurse. He married again and was separated within weeks. He married a third time and his house was destroyed by fire. Finally, his third wife bore him a healthy daughter—but Issa himself died, at 64, before he could see the little girl born.

My friend Richard, one of my closest pals in high school, upon receiving a diagnosis of prostate cancer three years ago, created a blog called "This world of dew." I sent him some information about Issa—whose poems, till his death, express almost nothing but gratitude for the beauties of life—but Richard died quickly and in pain, barely able to walk the last time I saw him.

My neighbors in Japan live in a culture that is based, at some invisible level, on the Buddhist precepts that Issa knew: that suffering is reality, even if unhappiness need not be our response to it. This makes for what comes across to us as uncomplaining hard work, stoicism and a constant sense of the ways difficulty binds us together—as Britain knew during the blitz, and other cultures at moments of stress, though doubly acute in a culture based on the idea of interdependence, whereby the suffering of one is the suffering of everyone.

"I'll do my best!" and "I'll stick it out!" and "It can't be helped" are the phrases you hear every hour in Japan; when a tsunami claimed thousands of lives north of Tokyo two years ago, I heard much more lamentation and panic in California than among the people I know around Kyoto. My neighbors aren't formal philosophers, but much in the texture of the lives they're used to—the national worship of things falling away in autumn, the blaze of cherry blossoms followed by their very quick departure, the Issa-like poems on which they're schooled—speaks for an old culture's training in saying goodbye to things and putting delight and beauty within a frame. Death undoes us less, sometimes, than the hope that it will never come.

As a boy, I'd learned that it's the Latin, and maybe a Greek, word for "suffering" that gives rise to our word "passion." Etymologically, the opposite of "suffering" is, therefore, "apathy"; the Passion of the Christ, say, is a reminder, even a proof, that suffering is something that a few high souls embrace to try to lessen the pains of others. Passion with the plight of others makes for "compassion."

Almost eight months after the Japanese tsunami, I accompanied the Dalai Lama to a fishing village, Ishinomaki, that had been laid waste by the natural disaster. Gravestones lay tilted at crazy angles when they had not collapsed altogether. What once, a year before, had been a thriving network of schools and homes was now just rubble. Three orphans barely out of kindergarten stood in their blue school uniforms to greet him, outside of a temple that had miraculously survived the catastrophe. Inside the wooden building, by its altar, were dozens of colored boxes containing the remains of those who had no surviving relatives to claim them, all lined up perfectly in a row, behind framed photographs, of young and old.

As the Dalai Lama got out of his car, he saw hundreds of citizens who had gathered on the street, behind ropes, to greet him. He went over and asked them how they were doing. Many collapsed into sobs. "Please change your hearts, be brave," he said, while holding some and blessing others. "Please help everyone else and work hard; that is the best offering you can make to the dead." When he turned round, however, I saw him brush away a tear himself.

Then he went into the temple and spoke to the crowds assembled on seats there. He couldn't hope to give them anything other than his sympathy and presence, he said; as soon as he heard about the disaster, he knew he had to come here, if only to remind the people of Ishinomaki that they were not alone. He could understand a little of what they were feeling, he went on, because he, as a young man of 23 in his home in Lhasa had been told, one afternoon, to leave his homeland that evening, to try to prevent further fighting between Chinese troops and Tibetans around his palace.

He left his friends, his home, even one small dog, he said, and had never in 52 years been back. Two days after his departure, he heard that his friends were dead. He had tried to see loss as opportunity and to make many innovations in exile that would have been harder had he still been in old Tibet; for Buddhists like himself, he pointed out, inexplicable pains are the result of karma, sometimes incurred in previous lives, and for those who believe in God, everything is divinely ordained. And yet, his tear reminded me, we still live in Issa's world of "And yet."

The large Japanese audience listened silently and then turned, insofar as its members were able, to putting things back together again the next day. The only thing worse than assuming you could get the better of suffering, I began to think (though I'm no Buddhist), is imagining you could do nothing in its wake. And the tear I'd witnessed made

me think that you could be strong enough to witness suffering, and yet human enough not to pretend to be master
of it. Sometimes it's those things we least understand that
deserve our deepest trust. Isn't that what love and wonder
tell us, too?

❦

7

I Found God in the Pain of My Brother's Suicide

Patrick T. Reardon

I found God in the pain of my brother's suicide.

I don't want to tell this story again—of my brother David, wracked with pain, dragging himself out his back door at 3 a.m. with rain-snow falling, to end his life with a gun.

David and I were the oldest of fourteen siblings. He was born a year and a month after me, and he had a bumpy, troubled life, with a lot of anger just beneath the surface. For years, he angrily lectured me, berated me, about politics and religion at family parties. It was a battering experience.

Then, in his 60s, he started to ease up a bit and then a lot. In 2015, he had extensive back surgery that left him very weak. Even worse, for a month, he was loopy on drugs he'd been given, and he hated being loopy, being out of control.

I don't want to think of this again. We were developing a tentative rekindling of our friendship, our brotherhood, when, out of the blue, the medicine that had kept his arthritis in check stopped working. He was in great pain, and a doctor he went to told him he needed four surgeries, one for each shoulder and knee—this to someone who, only months before, had gone through a horrific operation and recovery.

I talked with David just a few hours before he went out into the cold November darkness. I had never heard him so weak. I had never felt as close to him as I did then. I don't want to think about it again.

I didn't want to think of it again, but, through psychotherapy—a kind of prayer for me—I have thought of it again and again. And I thought about our childhood, and our parents, and the pain of our childhood, and the pain of our lives, his and mine. And that pain mixed with the sorrow of David's death, the grief at his despair.

And, in that pain, I saw—I realized—that God was there. I'm not talking about a voice from heaven or a vision or a cooling breeze. I'm talking that God was there, somehow, in the ripped and jagged, raw agony of facing these unfaceable experiences.

The God who was there with me as I moved deep and deeper into this pain wasn't the Jesus who called the little children to him, or who preached the Beatitudes. It was the Jesus of the cross, and the God of two dark, bleak books of the Old Testament—Ecclesiastes and Job.

Ecclesiastes begins with those famous lines: "Vanity of vanities . . . vanity of vanities! All things are vanity!"

Modern translators tell us that "vanity" isn't exactly the right word, and some versions have the opening words as "Everything is meaningless" or "Pointless! Pointless!" Famed translator of the Hebrew Bible Robert Alter renders it: "Merest breath . . . merest breath. All is mere breath," explaining that "mere breath" isn't the taking in of life-giving air, but the exhalation of the unusable vapor, the small quickly disappearing white cloud that is visible when you breathe out on a very cold day.

My life is as substantial as a cloud of vapor. David's life was. Here today, and then gone.

So why is Ecclesiastes, grim and stark as it is, even in the Bible? From the pain of David's death and the pain of my looking, for the first time in my life, full-face at many anguishing things, I have come to think that this is where God is and demands that I go—that I leap into this unknown. That despite the desolateness of life, I embrace the pain as, somehow, a route to faith and hope, a highway to God.

The only alternative, for me, is to run from pain and accept the desolateness of life. I don't want to do that.

On the cross, Jesus shouted, "My God, my God, why have you forsaken me?" He knew, at that moment, pain and desolation. His feelings of abandonment and isolation and loneliness and pain had pushed aside his hope and his faith. He was, as each of us is at times in our life, a raw nerve.

Later, though, Jesus accepted his desolation and accepted his death, saying, "Father, into thy hands I commend my spirit." It was an act of will, an act to push aside the emptiness and open himself to the mystery. Faith and hope are rooted in mystery, and what Jesus did at this moment is to embrace that mystery.

In this moment of greatest darkness, he commended himself to the Father; he trusted the Father, like a toddler who jumps out away from the couch, trusting that his mother will catch him as she has so many times before.

In Job, God tells that much-plagued righteous man to stop complaining and, in a wonderfully wild powerful poetic rant, essentially says to Job that he has no idea of the way things work. Only God does.

I embrace that unknown. Either I believe that God is here with me in these darkest moments—or desolation, all is desolation.

I don't know why good things happen to bad people and bad things happen to good people. I don't know why people I love have died from accidents and disease—and are dying. I don't know why I will live my entire life only to die. And I don't know why David killed himself.

I know, though, that I'm offered the choice to commend myself to God, to trust God, and to feel in some way that, at each dark moment, God is there with me in a way I don't understand and can't understand.

I have come to find that, like a toddler, I have to jump. So I do.

8

We Don't Take Her Breath for Granted

Tom Smith

I rolled over and said, "I hope you're able to sleep tonight."

She responded drowsily, "I think I will . . . once I can catch my breath."

Fran woke up three times during the night with long coughing spells. A respiratory illness can do that.

The lung issues emerged after her fourth and final chemo treatment for breast cancer eight years ago and, as she says, she's been living with "a hose in her nose" ever since. A 50-foot plastic cord connected to an oxygen-producing concentrator in our living room gives her access to our home, and I have learned the art of dodging the moving cord when we walk around the house.

"I want to be as active as I can for as long as I can," she announced on our way home from the hospital eight years ago. Fran is a woman of her word. "If it means that I die a few years earlier, then that's what it means."

Without trying to sound alarmist, I added, "Well, I believe in that principle but we need to draw the line on activity somewhere. I feel you're better off if you don't do. . . ."

Six years later, we're having that same conversation because it's not easy to make decisions about cutting back on activity, and we don't always agree.

The thing about the lungs is that they don't really get better. Once significantly damaged they don't revert to functioning like new again. The medications and breathing exercises are intended to prevent them from getting worse. And her illness is a progressively deteriorating disease. The idea is to slow down the decline.

"You know what I don't like," she says while I push her wheelchair in Kohl's looking for her new purse. "I don't like pity. I'm really grateful when people open doors and the disabled parking places are so helpful, but not pity. It makes me feel more helpless than I am."

I smiled when she said that, because Fran is definitely a fighter, always has been. She will fight for her clients (she still "sees" people in our home, helping them deal with a variety of personal and family issues). She will fight the weather to watch a grandson's soccer game. She will take vacations, give talks, attend meetings, lead support groups, follow the news, enjoy book club, play cards and games, visit people and, when possible, walk our treadmill. Her pulmonologist is amazed. I am too, frankly, but not surprised.

It is no wonder that breath is a symbol of God, the Holy Spirit. It's when she can't breathe that we don't take it for granted, and we know, really know, how essential it is. The all-pervasive, infiltrating presence of oxygen pumps life into our bodies. God indeed.

But her condition forces thoughts and talk about the future and death. As her limitations increase, "letting go" becomes more frequent, complex, real and necessary. "This is hard," she says, and I nod sadly because it is hard. For both of us.

Fran knows that letting go is a key to spiritual growth, to seeing life in its true perspective, in peeling things down to love, service, acceptance, forgiveness and joy. "But I can't let go of my breath that's being taken away from me. I know that in some way, I must let go of something, but not my breath."

Sometimes letting go of one thing means hanging on to something else.

"I think I have accepted my illness but then it evolves into something else, another level that I have to accept all over again."

Fran and I love to travel but it was mighty scary when we flew the last time and she couldn't get her blood oxygen level up to normal at 30,000 feet. Do we chance flying again? How do we decide? Just another limitation to accept?

Bronchitis sneaks into our home and leads to pneumonia, which squeezes more breath out of her. Lung capacity is down to 35 percent, and she walks slower and needs to sit in our living room on her way from the bedroom to the kitchen. As I get her "puffer," the always-present rescue inhaler, she insists, "I'm OK. I just need to breathe a little." It takes more than a month to recover from the bronchitis.

The doctor advises against going out in crowds for fear of infections, but our schedule includes church on Sunday, a movie on Tuesday morning, soccer game on Wednesday, the suicide survivor support group we run on Thursday, and bridge on Saturday.

She may send her "regrets" on something scheduled, but the principle remains: "I am not going to die before I'm dead."

Only one thing is as clear as the air we breathe: We are grateful for every breath she takes.

Sparks

To live is to suffer, to survive is to find
some meaning in the suffering.

—FRIEDRICH NIETZSCHE

If we do not transform our pain, we
will most assuredly transmit it—usually
to those closest to us: our family, our
neighbors, our co-workers, and invari-
ably, the most vulnerable, our children.

—RICHARD ROHR, OFM

Faith isn't about having everything
figured out ahead of time; faith is
about following the quiet voice of God
without having everything figured out
ahead of time.

—RACHEL HELD EVANS

9

I Hold His Hand

Steve Duin

If you stepped from the freight car holding your son's hand, you joined him in the showers. That was almost automatic. The kids went to the gas chambers first. If your fingers were entwined in your daughter's, you went along for the ride. The Nazis at Auschwitz or Treblinka didn't have time to pry you apart. The kinder guards working the railroad platforms would whisper, "Give away your baby," but what parent could heed that advice? They'd ferried the child that far. They'd kept their sons and daughters safe and reasonably well-fed in the ghetto and through the long, brutal haul of deportation. Why would they, how could they, let go of that hand?

It is early morning, and I am keeping a wary eye on my son, Michael. We have come to the Holocaust Memorial Museum, just a block from the Washington Monument, and I don't know if he is ready for what we will see. I'd also wanted to bring my seven-year-old daughter, Christina, but Mary Morrison, the museum's press liaison, told me she was just too young. "We don't recommend the exhibition for children under the age of eleven," she said. "But if he's mature nine-and-a-half . . ." Michael? Mature? How do I measure that? He's not old enough to go to 7-Eleven alone on his bike. He knows the NBA better than I do, but he's not ready for "Schindler's List."

Maybe I just want him with me. Four-foot high walls guard the view of some of the worst displays—the medical experiments and the films taken of the bodies and the bulldozers when the death camps were "liberated." Maybe I trust that I can choose what Michael sees and what he doesn't.

The museum doesn't give us much time to get ready. There is no warm-up lap. When the elevator takes you up to the fourth floor—the beginning of the long, slow decent into hell—and the doors open, you are met by a huge photograph from the concentration camp at Ohrdruf, Germany. It is April 1945, and the American soldiers have arrived. They are staring at a funeral pyre in which the burnt branches and blackened corpses are stacked like Lincoln Logs. Dwight Eisenhower was at Orhdruf. "The things I saw beggar description," he said. Neither do I know what to say as I turn to Michael.

"Do you know what that is?" I ask.

His hands are in his pockets, his eyes on the floor. "Yeah," he says, and we move on. I won't know for another two hours that the image is still burning inside him.

As we follow the exhibits making the rise of the Nazis, and the fall of the Jews, his questions come. Are the

concentration camp uniforms real? Why are they burning books? How did they hang all the photographs high
overhead in the Tower of Faces? Why didn't we bomb
Auschwitz?

Some questions I can answer, some I can't. Maybe it's
because Michael is with me, but I am pulled along by the
pictures and stories of children. They stare into the cameras
as if they are weapons. They are at the front of the line
in Mieczyslaw Stobierski's model of Crematorium II at
Auschwitz. Dr. Josef Mengele, I am told, did some of his
best work on kids.

Here is a photograph of a "mentally disabled" girl at
the asylum in Sonnenstein. She is 9, maybe 9½, and she is
naked. Her eyes are closed in pain; at her throat, keeping
her face turned toward the camera, are the fists of the nurse
whose face we cannot see. As the Nazis developed their
mass-killing machines, they tested the gas and the ovens on
the handicapped. This child was gone by 1941.

As our descent continues, I sometimes lose track of
my son. I am too involved to follow his retreat. Now and
then, I turn and see Michael in the distance, framed in the
doorway of the reconstructed Auschwitz barrack. Then he
returns, seeking shelter. I feel his head against my back as,
peering over the 4-foot high wall, I watch the firing squads
send fresh bodies tumbling in mass graves.

Michael is in more of a hurry than I am. I suspect that
he's rushing to get to the Wexner Learning Center at the
exhibit's end so he can play with the computers. But when
we're seated at a work station with our headphones on, I

feel him wince each time I touch the screen to call up another subject.

"No photos," he begs me. "There may be photos I don't like. That's why I don't want to stay."

And we don't.

Outside, the noon sun is so bright that it hurts our eyes. The wind is sharp and cold, and Michael is fishing for lunch. Can we stop for a bag of chips? When am I going to let him ride to 7-Eleven on his bike?

Riding on the Washington subway, he asks me which goes faster, Metro or MAX back home. We talk. We argue. He leans his head against my shoulder.

I hold his hand.

〰

10

Who Am I, Lord, That You Should Know My Name?

Bruce Lawrie

My six-year-old son and I share a nightly ritual, just the two of us alone in the fading light of his bedroom. Matty, who is severely mentally retarded, loves routine because life comes at him as if blasted from a water cannon, the millions of sights and sounds we all unconsciously assimilate every second of every day an undecipherable roar. Even more than most children, Matthew craves the safety that comes from learning the rhythms of his life, thrives on repetition. And of all his daily routines, winding down to bedtime might be the best. For a few minutes every night, I can turn down the white noise for him and help him ease into the peaceful joy of drifting off to sleep. We start out sitting on the floor with his favorite board book about monkeys drumming on drums, dumditty, dumditty, dum, dum, dum. . . . The book is worn with love, all four corners gnawed off—Matthew chews up books the way other kids do grilled-cheese sandwiches, starting at the corners and working his way to the center. As we reach the last dumditty on the last page, he lets out a sigh that tells me everything's right in his world and he's looking forward to climbing into bed.

I rise to my feet and begin singing, *Lord, I lift your name on high . . .* as I reach down to help him into bed.

He's unable to walk on his own but he can aim himself in the general direction of the bed. He knows where this is heading and he's ready for it. He pauses at the bedside to feel the blankets and pillow for a moment as if to make sure the bed is still stationary. Legally blind in one eye, he's learned that things have a disturbing way of disappearing right when you're ready to lean on them. But, as always, he finds the cool sheets safe, slings a skinny leg over the bed, and hauls himself up on top, moving rapidly before the bed can escape. He lies on his back rocking back and forth in bed, body rigid, a crease-eyed smile lighting his face, letting out an ecstatic aaahh.

I turn out the light and kneel beside his bed in the dark room, still singing, *You came from heaven to earth. . . .*

Matty holds his arm out in my direction, a tentative groping for me in the sudden blackness. I wrap his hand in mine and press it to my face. I start singing the next song in our nightly rotation as I brush his hand against my whiskers, first his palm and then the back of his hand. He explores my face with his fingertips and then he covers my mouth gently. I sing into his palm, imagining the reverberations vibrating down into his little soul. How does he experience me? What am I in his world? I don't know. I may never know.

I keep singing. *Only you can look inside me. . . .*

Who will care for Matty when I am gone? Who will keep him safe? Or maybe I'll outlive him. Many children like Matthew don't live out a normal life span. Would it be better if he went first? As is often the case with Matty, I don't have the answers. What I do have, though, is this moment in the dark with him, his soft hand gently brushing my lips, the source of the soothing song, the same song he's heard nearly every night of his six years on the planet. Those hazel eyes of his which so seldom look into mine are easing shut.

Who am I, Lord, that you should know my name?

I finish the song and stand up and wonder what heaven will be for my son. Maybe it'll be a place a lot like here, a place where his own son will run from him across a wide-open field of green, every nerve-end in his little body singing, where afterwards, Matty and I can tip back a beer together at a pub. Where he has a healthy body and a lovely wife and our family can linger long over pasta and homemade bread and salad and red wine. Where his son, my grandson, will fall asleep in my lap, a sweaty load of spent boy pinning me to my chair on the deck, the night sounds stirring around us, the stars rioting in the dark sky.

I look down on Matty's peaceful sleeping face. So often peace has eluded him: the operations, the I.V.s, the straps tying his hands to the hospital bed rails so he wouldn't pull the needles out, the countless blood draws when they couldn't find the vein, all the insults descending out of the blue onto my little boy who couldn't understand why the people around him had suddenly begun torturing him. But he is at peace right now. And a time is coming when he will have peace and have it to the full. And all the other things he's been robbed of. Meeting a girl. Playing catch with his father and his son. Making love. Calling his mother's name aloud. Talking with his twin sister. Eating a pizza. Drinking a beer. Running. And I'll get to be there with him. God will carve out a little slice of eternity for us, our own private do-over where the breeze carries the smell of fresh-cut grass, where the sky is bluer than you ever thought it could be, where the air feels newborn.

Soon, Matty. Soon.

🌿

God on the Gallows

Dorothee Soelle

How can hope be expressed in the face of senseless suffering?

I begin with a story that Elie Wiesel, a survivor of Auschwitz, relates in his book *Night*:

> The SS hung two Jewish men and a boy before the assembled inhabitants of the camp. The men died quickly but the death struggle of the boy lasted half an hour. "Where is God? Where is he?" a man behind me asked. As the boy, after a long time, was still in agony on the rope, I heard the man cry again, "Where is God now?" And I heard a voice within me answer, "Here he is—he is hanging here on this gallows."

It is difficult to speak about this experience. One has not yet traveled the way that leads from the question to the answer simply by reflecting on it theologically. The reflection stands in danger of missing the way itself since it is bound to other situations and thus cannot comprehend the question.

Within Jewish religious thinking the answer given here is understood in terms of the shekinah, the "indwelling presence of God in the world." According to cabalistic teaching God does not forsake the suffering world, in need of redemption after the fall. "His glory itself descends to the world, enters into it, into 'exile,' dwells in it, dwells with the troubled, the suffering creatures in the midst of their uncleanness—desiring to redeem them." In his emptied, abased form God shares the suffering of his people in exile, in prison, in martyrdom. Wandering, straying, dispersed, his indwelling rests in things and awaits the redemption of God through his creatures. God suffers where people suffer. God must be delivered from pain. "It is not merely in appearance that God has entered into exile in His indwelling in the world; it is not merely in appearance that in His indwelling He suffers with the fate of His world." So one can say that God, in the form of this shekinah, hangs on the gallows at Auschwitz and waits "for the initial movement toward redemption to come from the world. . . ." (Buber). Redemption does not come to people from outside or from above. God wants to use people in order to work on the completion of his creation. Precisely for this reason God must also suffer with the creation.

To interpret this story within the framework of the Christian tradition, it is Christ who suffers and dies here. To be sure, one must ask the effect of such an interpretation, which connects Christ with those gassed in Auschwitz and those burned with napalm in Vietnam. Wherever one compares the incomparable—for instance, the Romans' judicial murder of a first-century religious leader and the fascist genocide in the twentieth century—there, in a sublime manner, the issue is robbed of clarity, indeed the modern horror is justified. The point of view from which the comparison proceeds is not the number of victims nor the method of killing. A fifty-year-old woman piece worker hangs on the cross no less than Jesus—only longer. The only thing that can be compared is the person's relationship to the suffering laid upon him, his learning, his change. The justification for a Christian interpretation can only be established when it undergirds and clarifies what the story from Auschwitz contains.

In Jesus' passion history a decisive change occurs, the change from the prayer to be spared to the dreadfully clear awareness that that would not happen. The way from Gethsemane to Golgotha is a taking leave of (narcissistic) hope. It is the same change that occurs in the story from Auschwitz: the eye is directed away from the almighty Father to the sufferer himself. But not in such a way that this sufferer now has to endure everything alone. The essence of Jesus' passion history is the assertion that this one whom God forsook himself becomes God. Jesus does not die like a child who keeps waiting for his father. His "Eli, Eli" is a scream of growing up, the pain of this cry is a birth pang. When religion, which one can comprehend as the bundle of defense mechanisms against disappointment, intensifies one's holding fast to his father, then "faith [accomplishes] part of the task Freud assigns to whoever undertakes to 'do without his father . . . '" (Ricoeur).

The task of doing without one's father is accomplished in the story transmitted from Auschwitz, though to be sure in a way different from that in the mythical story of the death and resurrection of Christ. The mythical story is separated here, divided among individual voices. What Jesus experienced in himself is here assigned to three different characters. The man behind the narrator cries what Jesus cried; the boy died, as did Jesus; and the narrator hears a voice that tells him where God is, rather, who God is—the victim. But while Jesus is the question, victim, and answer in one person, in this story all communication breaks down. The questioner does not get the answer; the message does not reach the dying one, and the narrator remains alone with his voice, a fact one can scarcely endure.

The decisive phrase, that God is hanging "here on this gallows," has two meanings. First, it is an assertion about God. God is no executioner—and no almighty spectator (which would amount to the same thing). God is not the mighty tyrant. Between the sufferer and the one who causes the suffering, between the victim and the executioner, God, whatever people make of this word, is on the side of the sufferer. God is on the side of the victim, he is hanged.

Second, it is an assertion about the boy. If it is not also an assertion about the boy, then the story is false and one can forget about the first assertion. But how can the assertion about the boy be made without cynicism? "He is with God, he has been raised, he is in heaven." Such traditional phrases are almost always clerical cynicism with a high apathy content. Sometimes one stammers such phrases which are in fact true as a child repeats something he doesn't understand, with confidence in the speaker and the language that has still not become part of him. That is always possible, but in the long run it destroys those who do it because learning to believe also means learning to speak, and it is theologically necessary to transcend the shells of our inherited language. What language can possibly serve not only to preserve for all the life asserted by classical theology but primarily to translate it into a language of liberation? We would have to learn to hear the confession of the Roman centurion, "Truly this was God's son," in the phrase, "Here he is—he is hanging here on this gallows." Every single one of the six million was God's beloved son. Were anything else the case, resurrection would not have occurred, even in Jesus' case.

God is not in heaven; he is hanging on the cross. Love is not an otherworldly, intruding, self-asserting power—and to meditate on the cross can mean to take leave of that dream.

Precisely those who in suffering experience the strength of the weak, who incorporate the suffering into their lives, for whom coming through free of suffering is no longer the highest goal, precisely they are there for the others who, with no choice in the matter, are crucified in lives of senseless suffering. A different salvation, as the language of metaphysics could promise it, is no longer possible. The God who causes suffering is not to be justified even by lifting the suffering later. No heaven can rectify Auschwitz. But the God who is not a greater Pharaoh has justified himself: in sharing the suffering, in sharing the death on the cross.

God has no other hands than ours. Even "the future," which today is often supposed to translate the mythical word "heaven," cannot alter the fact that the boy had to die that way in Auschwitz. . . . But perhaps this future can preserve the memory of these children and thereby put up a better fight against death.

It is no less significant for us than it is for the boy that God is the one hanging on this gallows. God has no other hands than ours, which are able to act on behalf of other children.

The objection can be raised that even with this thought the dead are still "being used" for the living. They are to help us, to change us. That is perhaps true—but is any other relationship with the dead conceivable? Doesn't all remembering of them and all praying for them, all eating in remembrance of them have this character, that we "need" the dead in a double sense, of wanting them and of making use of them? They have been taken from us and are unable to prevent this use of themselves. But there is no way for us to love them other than to incorporate them into our work at living. There is no other way but to consume them—and perhaps that represents a debt we owed them that cannot be paid in life. Through our behavior we can turn them into "the devil's martyrs" posthumously, who confirm the eternal cycle of injustice under the sun and bring ourselves to speechlessness; or we can use them for praise to God.

In this sense those who suffer in vain and without respect depend on those who suffer in accord with justice. If there were no one who said, "I die, but I shall live," no one who said, "I and the Father are one," then there would be no hope for those who suffer mute and devoid of hoping. All suffering would then be senseless, destructive pain that could not be worked on, all grief would be "worldly grief" and would lead to death. But we know of people who have lived differently, suffered differently. There is a history of resurrections, which has vicarious significance. A person's resurrection is no personal privilege for himself alone—even if he is called Jesus of Nazareth. It contains within itself hope for all, for everything.

🌿

12

When I Knew:
Godlessness and God
on September 11

Patrick Giles

It wasn't when the first tower fell, or when I could hear—
on the phone with a friend who lived very close—the
second tower come clattering down.

It wasn't when I stood at 9th Avenue and 14th Street
to catch my breath, and by turning my head just an inch
to the right saw serene people safe in the beautiful light
and air, and then by turning my head just an inch to the
left saw a sky blackening with dust from the two buildings, and right before me silent tangles of people covered
by the detritus of coworkers and friends numbly trying to
find their way home.

It wasn't when I managed to get within a few blocks
of where those buildings had been, buildings I'd worked
in, and I was stopped by a young cop, who answered my
hoarse *don't you understand? There are thousands of*

people down there! With his Mister, I just saw, and there's
nobody down there, that I felt my soul roll its eyes to find
the grace of God.

But there was no sign of Him anywhere.

All those moments reminded me of others: the moment
when a concentration camp survivor described to me what
it was like to survive mass murder, to keep going when
the smoke of that day's dead palled the entire camp and
made breathing impossible; or the day during my AIDS
volunteering when four people with AIDS I had cared for
died within a few hours of each other, on the same floor
of the same hospital, and even the nurses were scrambling
from terror, the empty hospital hallway full of the sounds
of sobbing and slamming doors.

But that moment, on the street in New York on September 11, at that moment I felt again what I had on those
earlier days, I felt what I dreaded above everything else,
even death itself: at that moment I believed in Godlessness.

So, no, He never reached down to take my arm or lend
me his shoulder. The clouds refused to part. His voice
wasn't rolling anywhere, even amid squealing of collapsing
girders and shrieks of exploding glass that could be heard
from more than a mile away, or among the people getting
bottled water for wanderers on the street, some of them so
blanketed by ash they looked scorched, or among the people who didn't make it downtown running into a neighbor
or colleague who did, the neighbor or colleague raising
his voice to say Don't you understand? Hardly anybody
got out, I don't know how I made it, the others were all

still up there, or among the people camped out hopefully on stoops of friends' or lovers' houses eager for a reunion.

But something did happen later, downtown, just before twilight, when I was standing a half mile away from It, with hundreds of other people eager to help somebody, anybody. A young women whose face was still grayed by layers of ash stammered she had stood before the tower she'd worked in (trying not to be thankful a long line at the coffee shop had kept her outside) and forced herself to pray for each person she saw falling—I asked God to turn them into angels right away, before . . . and she paused, her sweet voice answered by a roar that maybe we both thought was some kind of attempt at an answer, even though it made the air itself cringe. Everybody turned heads south to see 7 or 11 WTC collapsing, and another giant cloud of debris swallowing block after block in seconds, hot on our trail. I remember the sound of hundreds of feet pounding north in an instant, of rushing and rushing forward as hard as I could, even though I held no hope anymore and as the first whoosh of hot pursuing air pushed forward on the asphalt to slow down our feet I found myself not minding that this might be the last feeling I'd ever know.

It still wasn't exactly then, either. It really began a moment later, when a hand grabbed my left arm and pulled (I was one of the slowest people in the crowd), and other people pulled slower ones along with them as they ran, and a voice like out of another older Fall trembled as it cried Don't look back!, and another hand reached amid the whirl of breaths and foot-beats towards mine to help me along, and a crunching, sucking sound shoved every other sound out of the way as I saw in windows of buildings alongside me the cloud getting nearer and nearer, but we kept running, and it stopped following us.

My lungs had given up the ghost, and as I searched for a sewer to stick my face into (someone else had done this when the first tower fell, and had told me about it). I tried not to look back, and muttered to hell with Lot's wife, and I turned to look back. The debris cloud was half a block away, hovering enormous and splendid and so full of the power of suffering I almost bowed before it; but just short of crossing the street it had paused, as if having consumed so much that was human it had learned politeness and was waiting for the traffic light to change (I could see around its edges two little red lights winking to green) before it came after us afresh. Or maybe, as the cloud just stayed where it was, it seemed as if some force bigger than evil had put a hand on the thing, made it pile upon itself up and up into the sky (as it was now doing, its ascending rumbles as shocking as enraged curses) rather than gallop forward to engulf us, because whatever had suddenly exercised restraint over it had spent the day watching thousands die and millions despair and had finally tossed omnipotence, forced a gap between more death and us, as if quietly but firmly saying to everything, enough.

That's when I thought at the time, amid the sound of hundreds of lungs wheezing with relief, and loud plops as bodies fell only a few feet to the gutter, not dead but crying and very alive. We weren't alone; we weren't abandoned; we weren't worthless and graceless; something or someone had stepped in and saved us; we could still live. Thank God, thank God, I heard a hundred times in ten seconds from inches or blocks away. But, I thought, a moment before I could thank God myself, and get up and start walking home again, Why can't I, even after a moment like this, ever be certain I really have anyone to thank?

❧

13

What I Really Want

Kate Bowler

This will be my first Christmas away from Canada, away from my church on the one night when all the wanderers who no longer attend return to hug one another and sing carols like only Mennonites can, in growly German and perfect four-part harmony. I have always loved the darkness and the candles during "Silent Night." Mostly I love the feeling of homecoming I get when I see Liz, who designed my prom dress in a shiny lavender poly-satin, and Ferd, who quietly nailed the cross back together after my friend and I accidentally broke it in an ill-advised reenactment of the crucifixion on a youth group overnight. I never told my parents and, God bless him, neither did Ferd. I look forward to getting a fierce hug from Charlotte, my mom's best friend, and my old Sunday school teacher Carol, who helped me get into my sheep costume for the Christmas pageant year after year.

A couple of Christmases ago, I saw Carol over one of the pews and reached out to give her a hug, remembering only at the last second that she had recently been diagnosed with cancer. I couldn't figure out what to say when we pulled away and I found I was just staring into her smiling face, stammering something about how sorry I was. She looked back at me with such calm and said something I had never heard anyone say.

"I have known Christ in so many good times," she said, sincerely and directly. "And now I will know Him better in His sufferings."

She meant it. And I could not imagine a world in which I could mean it. It was Christmas, and I was busy with presents, coffee dates, and rushing between family gatherings. It was only partway through the service that I began to hope that that Christmas feeling would sink in as the night gathered and the music slowed. The angels were singing and the Wise Men were on their way and all the church was ready for Jesus to be born, hut I hardly noticed. I wasn't asking God for anything in particular. Carol surely wanted healing and more years with her husband and an escape from the creeping death that is multiplying cells and the fading powers of chemotherapy drugs. And yet she prayed for more than to be saved. She prayed in the long night of Advent that her waiting would end with a better angle of vision on the baby born to die.

Toban encouraged me to put up the Christmas tree in October, and we trimmed the house with toasted pine-cones, bushy evergreen branches, and golden baubles. First thing in the morning, Zach loves to sprint from his room, his chubby arms pumping, to make sure he is there when

I flick on the lights to the tree. He laughs maniacally every time, tossing his head back with an evil "Ha! Ha! Ha!" like Vincent Price. I taught him how to do that, and I have never regretted it. Then he pulls a thick blanket over to where I am sitting and tucks us both into it. He looks up at me and smiles broadly.

God, I don't want to just know you better. I want to save my family.

Sparks

*Yea, though I walk through the valley
of the shadow of death, I will fear no
evil: for thou art with me; thy rod and
thy staff they comfort me.*

—Psalm 23:4

*Wither shall I go from thy spirit? Or
wither shall I flee from thy presence?
If I ascend up into heaven, thou art
there: if I make my bed in hell, behold
thou art there. If I take the wings of
the morning, and dwell in the utter-
most parts of the sea, even there shall
thy hand lead me and thy right hand
shall hold me.*

—Psalm 139:7–10

◖

14

I Thought I Knew Him: The Suffering Humanity of Christ

David J. Unger

We were still very new to the faith when my then-fiancée, Rachel, bought Magnificat's 2018 calendar and proposed we hang it on our kitchen wall. Neither she nor I had been raised in the church, and our largely secular upbringings had left us skeptical if not disdainful of Catholicism. The Catholic funeral of Rachel's grandfather, just ten months prior, had begun to change that. We started attending Mass. Rachel signed up for RCIA, and I reluctantly followed suit. Eventually, we grew so bold as to kneel in humility and pray together to the Lord.

The Magnificat calendar would be the first religious item to grace the walls of our illicit premarital home. This caused me some consternation. It was one thing to take a shine to the Gospel. It was something else entirely to proclaim it above the dishwasher. Finding yourself can feel eerily similar to losing yourself, and both inspire tremendous amounts of fear. I felt that fear as we nailed the Magnificat calendar to our kitchen wall.

My own path to belief would not come from a single epiphany, but instead grew out of little openings into extrasensory understanding. The start of February delivered one of these micro-revelations to me, as Rachel flipped the Magnificat calendar from January's *Christ and John the Baptist as Children* by Bartolomé Esteban Murillo to February's *The Temptation in the Wilderness* by Briton Rivière.

In that painting the Son of Man slumps alone on a rock in the empty desert. He steadies himself with his palms placed at either side. His downward gaze masks his face. The sun sets behind him, and a single star shines just above his sunken head. The whole painting seems to tremble and glow.

Christ grapples with both the fact of a human body and the presence of a human mind.

To see Christ like that for the first time was, for me, disarming; the painting robbed me of the tools I had used to ignore or dismiss him. Foremost among them was a conviction that I already knew Christ, and that he offered nothing for me. I thought I knew him because I had seen my grandparents' crucifixes. I had toured great European cathedrals. I had laughed at television's enlightened caricatures. I thought I knew Christ, but all I really knew was a cliché.

Rivière's painting contained none of the usual baggage, and thus contained all of Christ for me. Stripped of everything I knew about him, I could finally set about knowing him. I could see the creator of the universe take on human form and experience his creation as we experience it.

When the Word took on flesh, he took on consciousness, too. In Rivière's painting, Christ grapples with both the fact of a human body and the presence of a human mind. He's all alone there, as Thomas Merton put it, in a "sterile paradise of emptiness and rage" lorded over by the devil. He spent forty days there, staving off temptation, discerning his way toward a tortured end. The cross is as psychic as it is physical.

That resonated with me. I have never been spat upon or flogged. Nobody has pounded wrought-iron fasteners through my flesh. It has been easy for me to intellectualize away Christ's bodily passion. But I have known psychic pain—torment more spiritual than physical. So it was comforting for me, especially in the trying winter of my first Lent, to understand God as intimately familiar with the human mind, with how it can fold in upon itself in doubt, confusion, and fear. I may never fully understand why a benevolent God permits suffering, but I am steadied by his firsthand experience of it.

Months passed. Magnificat curated more beautiful paintings above our dishwasher. Previously, they would have stimulated only my academic sensibility. Now I find in them something raw. Christ, for me, is no longer a cliché held at arm's length, but someone real, someone with whom to cultivate a relationship. My conversion has been an exercise in reduction—as much about dislodging default assumptions as it is about embracing a revealed truth. To encounter Christ today, I have to cross a desert of my own ironic detachment.

Rachel and I were received into the church at Easter and Pentecost respectively. We were graced with yet another sacrament at our nuptial Mass on the Feast of St. Clare. It was indeed a year full of grace, and we are settling into a happy new life together. But on bad days, when things do not go my way, whenever I ask why God has forsaken me, it steadies me to know that He wondered the same thing, too.

〰

15

Love Leads to Suffering, But We Take the Risk to Love Because We Must

Heidi Russell

"God never promised us that we would not suffer." Those words struck a painful, but truthful, chord in me when a friend uttered them as we stood talking at the wake of a 27-year-old woman, a mother of a one-year-old and wife who died of cancer way too young.

We stood there witnessing the pain one instinctively feels no one should ever have to endure, if our God is a loving God—if, in fact, our God is love. And yet the reality is that Christianity does not teach us that we will not suffer. The opposite is true. Love leads to suffering.

Buddhism recognizes this great truth in the teaching of the Four Noble Truths, and one is encouraged to love without attachment, without desire, without trying to hold on to what or who we love. Christianity also teaches that to love is to suffer—to suffer for and with others, exemplified in the crucified Christ who stretched out his arms and died for love. God's response to our suffering is to suffer with us on the cross and to resurrect that suffering into new life. Still, knowing all of that, I could not be anything but devastated by the untimely death of this young woman. How could I trust God in the face of such tragedy?

I had not fully realized, prior to that point, that my idea of God was a God who fixed things, who would make things turn out all right in the end. That image of God, I discovered, is the God of the privileged, the God of those who have not suffered. I find since then, when I talk to people, there is a divide in how people know God—those who have suffered great tragedy and those who have not. To paraphrase C.S. Lewis, suffering is "the great iconoclast"—my idols could not hold up.

In his book *The Eternal Year*, theologian Karl Rahner suggests that when one experiences the absence of God, one's image of God is no longer working. The only way to rebuild trust in the face of such absence is to let go of the image and surrender to the mystery. God as love does not promise that we will not suffer. God promises us that when we do suffer, we are held in love. God does not promise to fix what is broken; God promises to be present in the midst of the brokenness.

That source of love we call God is revealed in the person of Jesus Christ, the word of love among us, and in the Holy Spirit, God as love enacted within us and among us. The only antidote to the brokenness of the world is to surrender to love, to let that love act in us and through us, even when we know it may ultimately lead to heartbreak.

Love and trust in a finite world are doomed to disappointment. Beyond the inevitable experience of death, our lives are also littered with broken promises, betrayals, people in their humanness letting us down time and again, or perhaps our own humanness and brokenness leading us to sabotage our relationships. We experience this human brokenness in our lovers, our families and our friends.

So the real question becomes, how is it that we continue to go on loving? Why do we continue to take the chance with our hearts to trust again, to give someone a second chance, or to start all over again with someone new? Rahner suggests that our desire to trust another human being wholly is fulfilled in the person of Jesus Christ. One who loves a fallible human being in some way affirms the one human person who does not disappoint, who is the perfect expression of God as Love in the world.

Scripture tells us we love because God first loves us (1 John 4:19). Humans cannot exist without love. God created us to be in relationship, to love. Psychology and neuroscience have demonstrated what mystics have taught us to perceive with the eye of the soul: that we are hardwired for love. Our brains have a whole pharmacy of neurochemicals that facilitate love, desire and attachment, and enable us to experience trust, generosity, altruism and empathy. Judith Horstman in *The Scientific American Book of Love, Sex and the Brain: The Neuroscience of How, When, Why and Who We*

Love, explains how in brain imaging research, it can be seen that love "lights up" our brains.

As interesting as the parts of the brain that are active, according to Horstman, are the parts that tend to be less active: fear, grief and self-protection. So when we read in Scripture that perfect love casts out fear (1 John 4:18), there is a truth to that statement on a physical as well as spiritual level. Love indeed does drive out fear. Thus the very way our brain works helps us continue to risk love in an era of distrust. Love, a spiritual realization, manifests and becomes the antidote for distrust.

We continue to love because we must, if we are going to be human. My relationship with God is now changed, but the relationship endures. I don't expect God to "fix" things anymore. The miracle for which I now pray is not to have the outcome of the story changed, but rather how I might manifest God's love in the midst of the grief and suffering of the world. My relationship to God as Love is manifested in my ability to love others, to love my neighbor as myself. God as source and ground of our love enables us to continue taking the risk to love, even when we have been devastated by love in the past.

And so we take the risk again and again to love other human beings, despite their tendency to disappoint and to die, and to love God who has enabled us to love by first loving us.

🌿

16

Why We Shouldn't Be Afraid of Suffering

Thich Nhat Hanh

We should not be afraid of suffering. We should be afraid of only one thing, and that is not knowing how to deal with our suffering. Handling our suffering is an art. If we know how to suffer, we suffer much less, and we're no longer afraid of being overwhelmed by the suffering inside. The energy of mindfulness helps us recognize, acknowledge, and embrace the presence of the suffering, which can already bring some calm and relief.

When a painful feeling comes up, we often try to suppress it. We don't feel comfortable when our suffering surfaces, and we want to push it back down or cover it up. But as a mindfulness practitioner, we allow the suffering to surface so we can clearly identify it and embrace it. This will bring transformation and relief. The first thing we have to do is accept the mud in ourselves. When we recognize and accept our difficult feelings and emotions, we begin to feel more at peace. When we see that mud is something that can help us grow, we become less afraid of it.

When we are suffering, we invite another energy from the depths of our consciousness to come up: the energy of mindfulness. Mindfulness has the capacity to embrace our suffering. It says, Hello, my dear pain. This is the practice of recognizing suffering. Hello, my pain. I know you are there, and I will take care of you. You don't need to be afraid.

Now in our mind-consciousness there are two energies: the energy of mindfulness and the energy of suffering. The work of mindfulness is first to recognize and then to embrace the suffering with gentleness and compassion. You make use of your mindful breathing to do this. As you breathe in, you say silently, Hello, my pain. As you breathe out, you say, I am here for you. Our breathing contains within it the energy of our pain, so as we breathe with gentleness and compassion, we are also embracing our pain with gentleness and compassion.

When suffering comes up, we have to be present for it. We shouldn't run away from it or cover it up with consumption, distraction, or diversion. We should simply recognize it and embrace it, like a mother lovingly embracing a crying baby in her arms. The mother is mindfulness, and the crying baby is suffering. The mother has the energy of gentleness and love. When the baby is embraced by the mother, it feels comforted and immediately suffers less, even though the mother does not yet know exactly what the problem is. Just the fact that the mother is embracing the baby is enough to help the baby suffer less. We don't need to know where the suffering is coming from. We just need to embrace it, and that already brings some relief. As our suffering begins to calm down, we know we will get through it.

When we go home to ourselves with the energy of mindfulness, we're no longer afraid of being overwhelmed by the energy of suffering. Mindfulness gives us the strength to look deeply and gives rise to understanding and compassion.

17

The Search for God Is a Search for Light

Marianne Williamson

Simply waking up in the morning and going through the daily routines of a normal existence can be emotionally or even physically burdensome. Excruciating pain can weigh upon the heart for months or even years, obliterating all joy and making the slightest comforts impossible. Traumatic memories can cut the psyche like razors. Suffering can overwhelm all else, and even if we think there is a God, He can seem at such moments like He is very far away.

But God is never far away, because God is in our minds. We are free to think whatever we wish to think. The door to emotional deliverance is primarily a mental one. By aligning our thoughts with His thoughts, we can awaken to Him in the midst of our suffering. We can find Him in the midst of our darkness. And we can walk with Him into the light that lies beyond. The universe is wired for God's light the way a house is wired for electricity, and every mind is like a lamp. But a lamp must be plugged in for it to shed any light. With every prayer, we plug in to the light. With every realization of our mistakes and willingness to atone for them, we plug in to the light. With every apology we give and receive, we plug in to the light. With every act of forgiveness, we plug in to the light. With every thought of mercy, we plug in to the light. With every moment of faith, we plug in to the light.

The search for God is a search for light, and outside that light we are sorrowful indeed. With it, we are healed and made whole.

🌿

18

The Thing Is

Ellen Bass

to love life, to love it even
when you have no stomach for it
and everything you've held dear
crumbles like burnt paper in your
     hands,
your throat filled with the silt of it.
When grief sits with you, its tropical
     heat
thickening the air, heavy as water
more fit for gills than lungs;
when grief weights you like your own
     flesh
only more of it, an obesity of grief,
you think, How can a body withstand
     this?
Then you hold life like a face
between your palms, a plain face,

no charming smile, no violet eyes,
and you say, yes, I will take you
I will love you, again.

Sparks

Christ has no body on earth but ours,
no hands but ours, no feet but ours.
Ours are the eyes through which the
compassion of Christ looks out upon
the world, ours are the feet with which
he goes about doing good, ours are the
hands with which he blesses his people.

—St. Teresa of Avila

Then I saw a new heaven and a new
earth, for the old heaven and the old
earth had disappeared.

—Revelation 21:1

PART TWO

OUT OF DARKNESS, LIGHT

Here comes the sun.

—GEORGE HARRISON

19

Miracles Happen

Marianne Williamson

We all face times in our lives when the pain of existence seems too much to bear. For some of us, these experiences happen rarely, and when they do, the pain is relatively mild. But for others of us, excruciating pain can weigh us down and make the slightest comfort difficult to achieve. Deeper and deeper we fall into the well of our own tears, into a darkness that seems to have no bottom. We wonder where all this suffering comes from. And we wonder whether it will ever end.

If you, or someone you love, are living through one of those times—feeling that to take another breath, even to live another day, seems hard to contemplate—then I'm glad you are reading this book [*Tears to Triumph*]. You may find here some pieces of the puzzle you have not yet explored. A mystery. Perhaps a miracle.

This doesn't mean that you won't have to make any effort. Miracles aren't a quick fix, or an easy answer. But they activate a spiritual power divinely authorized to help you.

God is here, even here, in the midst of your suffering. And as you reach out to Him, He will reach back.

Consider the possibility now that anything could happen. I'm not asking you to believe this, but only to consider that it might be true. Simply thinking this thought—that miracles are possible—does more to pave the way for your healing than you can imagine. It opens the door to a realm of infinite possibilities, regardless of what you have been through or what you are going through now.

The pain you are going through is not what will determine your future; your future will be determined by *who you are* as you go through your pain. This is not to question the depth of your suffering. Within the mortal world, it is certainly real. But the reality in which you are ensnared is not itself what it appears to be, nor are you yourself quite the being you feel you are now. We can expand the definition of who you are, as well as what the world is—and your life will begin to change. Your human self might be in hell right now, but your divine self is literally untouched by your suffering. And your divine self is who you are.

Your subconscious mind is aware of your larger reality and will assume the role of showing it to you when you are ready for it to do so. This process will be one of the great journeys of your life, as you will see things you haven't seen and know things you haven't known. Your tears, your hopelessness, your fear, your anger, your guilt, your resentment, your remorse, your terror—none of these will be papered over or denied. You will not dissolve them by keeping them in the dark, but by exposing them to the light. And as you do, you will see beyond them such magnificence—in yourself and in the world—that you will actually bless the journey of your suffering, for it led you to yourself and to the meaning of your life. Spiritual healing doesn't lie in denying your pain, but in feeling it fully and surrendering it to God.

And then the miracles begin . . .

20

There's Something Deeper Happening Here

Richard Rohr, OFM

All healthy religion shows you what to do with your pain, with the absurd, the tragic, the nonsensical, the unjust and the undeserved—all of which eventually come into every lifetime. If only we could see these "wounds" as *the way through,* as Jesus did, then they would become sacred wounds rather than scars to deny, disguise, or project onto others. I am sorry to admit that I first see my wounds as an obstacle more than a gift. Healing is a long journey.

If we cannot find a way to make our wounds into sacred wounds, we invariably become cynical, negative, or bitter. This is the storyline of many of the greatest novels, myths, and stories of every culture. *If we do not transform our pain, we will most assuredly transmit it*—usually to those closest to us: our family, our neighbors, our co-workers, and, invariably, the most vulnerable, our children.

Scapegoating, exporting our unresolved hurt, is the most common storyline of human history. The Jesus Story is about radically transforming history and individuals so that we don't just keep handing on the pain to the next generation. Unless we can find a meaning for human suffering, that *God is somehow in it* and can also use it for good, humanity is in major trouble. Because we *will* suffer. Even the Buddha said that suffering is part of the deal!

We shouldn't try to get rid of our own pain until we've learned what it has to teach. When we can hold our pain consciously and trustfully (and not project it elsewhere), we find ourselves in a very special liminal space. Here we are open to learning and breaking through to a much deeper level of faith and consciousness. Please trust me on this. We must all *carry the cross of our own reality* until God transforms us through it. *These are the wounded healers of the world, and healers who have fully faced their wounds are the only ones who heal anyone else.*

As an example of holding the pain, picture Mary standing at the foot of the cross or, as in Michelangelo's *Pietà* cradling Jesus' body. One would expect her to take her role wailing or protesting, but she doesn't! We must reflect on this deeply. Mary is in complete solidarity with the mystery of life and death. It's as if she is saying, "There's something deeper happening here. How can I absorb it just as Jesus is absorbing it, instead of returning it in kind?" Consider the analogy of energy circuits: Most of us are relay stations; only a minority are *transformers*—people who actually change the electrical charge that passes through us.

Jesus on the cross and Mary standing beneath the cross are classic images of transformative spirituality. They do not return the hostility, hatred, accusations, or malice directed at them. They hold the suffering until it becomes resurrection! That's the core mystery of Christianity. It takes our whole life to begin to comprehend this. It tends to be the wisdom of elders, not youngers.

Unfortunately, our natural instinct is to try to fix pain, to control it, or even, foolishly, to try to understand it. The ego insists on understanding. That's why Jesus praises a certain quality even more than love, and he calls it *faith*. It is the ability to stand in liminal space, to stand on the threshold, to hold the contraries, until we are moved by grace to a much deeper level and a much larger frame, where our private pain is not center stage but a mystery shared with every act of bloodshed and every tear wept since the beginning of time. Our pain is not just our own.

❧

21

It's a Gift to Exist

Stephen Colbert

In a CNN interview on August 15th, 2019, Anderson Cooper and Stephen Colbert were speaking about the untimely deaths of Colbert's father and two brothers, and the deep suffering he experienced. Cooper reminded Colbert of another interview on suffering where he had said that he had come to "love the things that I most wish had not happened."

Holding back tears, Cooper, whose mother had recently died, continued, "You went on to say, 'What punishments of God are not gifts?' Do you really believe that?"

Colbert's compassionate response was: "Yes. It's a gift to exist, and with existence comes suffering. There's no escaping that. I guess I'm either a Catholic or a Buddhist when I say those things because I've heard those from both traditions. . . . If you are grateful for your life . . . then you have to be grateful for all of it. You can't pick and choose what you're grateful for."

"So what do you get from loss? You get awareness of other people's loss, which allows you to connect with that other person, which allows you to love more deeply and to understand what it's like to be a human being, if it is true that all humans suffer."

"At a young age, I suffered something, so that by the time I was in serious relationships in my life, with friends, or with my wife or with my children, [I understood] that everybody is suffering. And however imperfectly, to acknowledge their suffering to connect with them, and to love them in a deep way that not only accepts that all of us suffer, but makes you grateful for the fact that *you* have suffered, so you can know that about other people."

"It's about the fullness of your humanity. What's the point of being here and being human if you can't be the most human you can be? . . . I want to be the most human I can be, and that involves acknowledging and ultimately being grateful for the things I wish didn't happen, because they gave me a gift."

Colbert later added, "In my tradition, that's the great gift of the sacrifice of Christ—that God does it too. You're really not alone. God does it too."

22

Spiritual Awakening and Intense Suffering

Eckhart Tolle

Since ancient times the term awakening has been used as a kind of metaphor that points to the transformation of human consciousness. There are parables in the New Testament that speak of the importance of being awake, of not falling back to sleep. The word Buddha comes from the Sanskrit word Budh, meaning, "to be awake." So Buddha is not a name and ultimately not a person, but a state of consciousness. All this implies that humans are potentially capable of living in a state of consciousness compared to which normal wakefulness is like sleeping or dreaming. This is why some spiritual teachings use terms like "shared hallucination" or "universal hypnotism" to describe normal human existence. Pick up any history book, and I suggest you begin with studying the 20th century, and you will find that a large part of the history of our species has all the characteristics we would normally associate with a nightmare or an insane hallucination.

The nature of spiritual awakening is frequently misunderstood. The adoption of spiritual beliefs, seeing visions of God or celestial beings, the ability to channel, to heal, to foretell the future, or other paranormal powers—all such phenomena are of value and are not to be dismissed, but none of them is in itself indicative of spiritual awakening in a person who experiences them. They may occur in a person who has not awakened spiritually and they may or may not accompany the awakened state.

Every morning we awaken from sleep and from our dreams and enter the state we call wakefulness. A continuous stream of thoughts, most of them repetitive, characterizes the normal wakeful state. So what is it that we awaken from when spiritual awakening occurs? We awaken from identification with our thoughts. Everybody who is not awake spiritually is totally identified with and run by their thinking mind—the incessant voice in the head. Thinking is compulsive: you can't stop, or so it seems. It is also addictive: you don't even want to stop, at least not until the suffering generated by the continuous mental noise becomes unbearable. In the unawakened state you don't use thought, but thought uses you. You are, one could almost say, possessed by thought, which is the collective conditioning of the human mind that goes back many thousands of years. You don't see anything as it is, but distorted and reduced by mental labels, concepts, judgments, opinions and reactive patterns. Your sense of identity, of self, is reduced to a story you keep telling yourself in your head. "Me and my story": this is what your life is reduced to in the unawakened state. And when your life is thus reduced, you can never be happy for long, because you are not yourself.

Does that mean you don't think anymore when you awaken spiritually? No, of course not. In fact, you can use thought much more effectively than before, but you realize there is a depth to your being, a vibrantly alive stillness that is much vaster than thought. It is consciousness itself, of which the thinking mind is only a tiny aspect. For many people, the first indication of a spiritual awakening is that they suddenly become aware of their thoughts. They become a witness to their thoughts, so to speak. They are not completely identified with their mind anymore and so they begin to sense that there is a depth to them that they had never known before.

For most people, spiritual awakening is a gradual process. Rarely does it happen all at once. When it does, though, it is usually brought about by intense suffering. That was certainly true in my case. For years my life alternated between depression and acute anxiety. One night I woke up in a state of dread and intense fear, more intense than I had ever experienced before. Life seemed meaningless, barren, hostile. It became so unbearable that suddenly the thought came into my mind, "I cannot live with myself any longer." The thought kept repeating itself several times. Suddenly, I stepped back from the thought, and looked at it, as it were, and I became aware of the strangeness of that thought: "If I cannot live with myself, there must be two of me—the

I and the self that I cannot live with." And the question arose, "Who is the 'I' and who is the self that I cannot live with?" There was no answer to that question, and all thinking stopped. For a moment, there was complete inner silence. Suddenly I felt myself drawn into a whirlpool or a vortex of energy. I was gripped by an intense fear, and my body started to shake. I heard the words, "Resist nothing," as if spoken inside my chest. I could feel myself being sucked into a void. Suddenly, all fear disappeared, and I let myself fall into that void. I have no recollection of what happened after that.

The next morning I awoke as if I had just been born into this world. Everything seemed fresh and pristine and intensely alive. A vibrant stillness filled my entire being. As I walked around the city that day, the world looked as if it had just come into existence, completely devoid of the past. I was in a state of amazement at the peace I felt within and the beauty I saw without, even in the midst of the traffic. I was no longer labeling and interpreting my sense perceptions—an almost complete absence of mental commentary. To this day, I perceive and interact with the world in this way: through stillness, not through mental noise. The peace that I felt that day, more than 20 years ago, has never left me, although it has varying degrees of intensity.

At the time, I had no conceptual framework to help me understand what had happened to me. Years later, I realized that the acute suffering I felt that night must have forced my consciousness to withdraw from identification with the unhappy self, the suffering "little me," which is ultimately a fiction of the mind. This withdrawal must have been so complete that the suffering self collapsed as if the plug had been pulled out of an inflatable toy. What was left was my true nature as the ever present "I AM": consciousness in its pure state prior to identification with form. You may also call it pure awareness or presence.

🌿 🌿 🌿

When you are trapped in a nightmare, your motivation to awaken will be so much greater than that of someone caught up in a relatively pleasant dream. On all levels, evolution occurs in response to a crisis situation, not infrequently a life-threatening one, when the old structures, inner or outer, are breaking down or are not working anymore. On a personal level, this often means the experience of loss of one kind or another: the death of a loved one, the end of a close relationship, loss of possessions, your home, status, or a breakdown of the external structures of your life that provided a sense of security. For many people, illness—loss of health—represents the crisis situation that triggers an awakening. With serious illness comes awareness of your own mortality, the greatest loss of all.

For many people alive at this time, loss is experienced as loss of meaning. In other words, life seems to lack purpose and doesn't make sense anymore. Loss of meaning is often part of the suffering that comes with physical loss, but it can also happen to people who have gained everything the world has to offer—who have "made it" in the eyes of the world—and suddenly find that their success or possessions are empty and unfulfilling. What the world and the surrounding culture tells them is important and of value turns out to be empty and this leaves a kind of painful inner void, often accompanied by great mental confusion.

Now the question arises: What exactly is the connection between suffering and spiritual awakening? How does one lead to the other? When you look closely at the nature of human suffering you will find that an essential ingredient in most kinds of suffering is a diminishment of one's sense of self. Take illness, for example. Illness makes you feel smaller, no longer in control, helpless. You seem to lose your autonomy, perhaps become dependent on others. You become reduced in size, figuratively speaking. Any major loss has a similar effect: some form that was an important part of your sense of who you are—a person, a possession, a social role—dissolves or leaves you and you suffer because you had become identified with it and it seems you are losing yourself or a part of yourself. In reality, of course, what feels like a diminishment or loss of your sense of self is the crumbling of an image of who you are held in the mind. What dissolves is identification with thought forms that had given you your sense of self. But that sense of self is ultimately false, is ultimately a mental fiction. It is the egoic mind or the "little me" as I sometimes call it. To be identified with a mental image of who you are is to be unconscious, to be unawakened spiritually. This unawakened state creates suffering, but suffering creates the possibility of awakening. When you no longer resist the diminishment of self that comes with suffering, all role-playing, which is normal in the unawakened state, comes to an end. You become humble, simple, real. And, paradoxically, when you say "yes" to that death, because that's what it is, you realize that the mind-made sense of self had obscured the truth of who you are—not as defined by your past, but timelessly. And when who you think you are dissolves, you connect with a vast power which is the essence of your very being. Jesus called it: "eternal life." In Buddhism, it is sometimes called the "deathless realm."

Now, does this mean that if you haven't experienced intense suffering in your life, there is no possibility of awakening? Firstly, the fact that you are drawn to a spiritual teaching or teacher means you must have had your share of suffering already, and the awakening process has probably already begun. A teacher or teaching is not even essential for spiritual awakening, but they save time. Secondly, humanity as a whole has already gone through unimaginable suffering, mostly self-inflicted, the culmination of which was the 20th century with its unspeakable horrors. This collective suffering has brought upon a readiness in many human beings for the evolutionary leap that is spiritual awakening. For many individuals alive now, this means: they have suffered enough. No further suffering is necessary. The end of suffering: that is also the essence of every true spiritual teaching. Be grateful that your suffering has taken you to this realization: I don't need to suffer anymore.

Sparks

One doesn't ask of one who suffers:
what is your country and what is your
religion? One merely says, You suffer.
This is enough for me. You belong to
me and I shall help you.

—LOUIS PASTEUR

There is no love which does not become
help.

—PAUL TILLICH

The less you open your heart to others,
the more your heart suffers.

—DEEPAK CHOPRA

❦

23

Learning to Suffer

Robert Ellsberg

*For the saint, suffering continues to be
suffering, but it ceases to be an obstacle
to his mission, or to his happiness, both
of which are found positively and con-
cretely in the will of God.*

—Thomas Merton

It may seem foolish to speak of suffering in connection
with the pursuit of happiness. Surely happiness—whatever
the word implies—requires the greatest possible distance
between ourselves and everything that hurts. Were it otherwise, we might be inclined to "pass." Yet suffering will
come to us all the same.

It is not astonishing to learn that we can find happiness through work, through love, through inner peace, or
detachment from everyday cares. Each of these pursuits,
after all, implies a certain contentment. But to say that we
shall be happy if only we learn to be content is a mere

tautology. Our contentment is thin fare if it can be undone by a flea, a spark, a patch of ice, a broken twig. And so it is here that we most need the guidance of the saints. For they have known a path to happiness on which suffering is no necessary impediment.

The saints do not teach us how to avoid suffering; they teach us how to suffer. They do not provide the "meaning" of suffering. But they lived by the assurance that there is a meaning or truth at the heart of life that suffering is powerless to destroy. They found that there is no place that is literally "godforsaken," but that in every situation, even the most grim and painful, there is a door that leads to love, to fullness of life . . . to happiness. This is the deepest mystery of the gospel. Our task, if we would learn from the saints, is to find that door and enter in.

🌿 🌿 🌿

We use only a small portion of our brain. There are muscles in our body that atrophy for lack of exercise. And there are, similarly, portions of our humanity that remain dormant and undiscovered until certain experiences come along—like falling in love, having a child, or facing death—that bring them to life. Suffering is surely one of these experiences. Léon Bloy, the French Catholic novelist, wrote, "In his poor heart man has places which do not yet exist and into them enters suffering in order to bring them to life."

Are they worth the price—these not-yet-existent places in the heart? We all know that suffering does not necessarily make us holy or even nice. It is just as likely to foster bitterness, self-pity, and cynicism. It is a serious error to imagine that suffering in itself is ever "good." But it can be productive. If our definition of happiness requires the absolute avoidance of suffering, then any pain or frustration is an obstacle to our goal. But the saints saw their goal differently. Most of them would have endorsed the words of St. Ignatius in his Spiritual Exercises, that human beings are "created to praise, reverence, and serve God" and by this means to attain eternal life. To the extent that we fulfill this mission we achieve our happiness. And toward this goal, it so happens, suffering is no impediment. It may even be an ally.

Friedrich Nietzsche wrote, "What does not destroy me makes me stronger." The saints, for their part, did not prize strength as much as compassion. As a plow breaks open hardened soil so that it can receive more water, so suffering can break open hardened hearts and make them receptive to deeper wisdom. In that light, what does not destroy us may make us better able to bear God's image.

🌿 🌿 🌿

Pierre Teilhard de Chardin, a French Jesuit and mystic, wrote about the constructive impact of suffering and failure: "The lives of the saints and, generally speaking, the lives of all those who have been outstanding for intelligence or goodness are full of these instances in which one can see the person emerging ennobled, tempered, and renewed from some ordeal, or even some downfall, which seemed bound to diminish or lay him low forever. Failure in that case plays for us the part that the elevator plays for an aircraft or the pruning knife for a plant. It canalizes the sap of our inward life, disengages the purest 'components' of our being in such way as to make us shoot up higher and straighter."

As a theologian and paleontologist, Teilhard sought to reconcile the cosmic mysticism of St. Paul with the insights of evolution and contemporary cosmology. His scientific imagination led him to see life and the universe in the widest possible perspective: the explosion of stars, the violent formation of great landmasses, and the tectonic shifts that resulted in mountains and canyons.

Teilhard believed it is possible to discern a similar process in the life of individuals, a principle of humanization that enables us to achieve our highest spiritual potential—in other words, to become holy. In this process we are formed not only by our conscious choices but also, and perhaps to a greater extent, by what we undergo involuntarily. He called this the principle of passive diminishment. It includes all the bits of ill fortune in our lives: "the barrier which blocks our way, the wall that hems us in . . . all the incidents and accidents of varying importance and varying kinds, the tragic interferences . . . which come between the world of 'other' things and the world that radiates out from us." But it also includes the passage of time, the gradual deterioration of old age, "little by little robbing us of ourselves and pushing us on toward the end." Teilhard believed that we are shaped and measured by our defeats as well as by our achievements; by our weaknesses as well as our strengths; by what we do and by what we endure. Both joy and suffering unleash spiritual energies that connect us to the divine center of reality.

🌿 🌿 🌿

Among those touched by Teilhard's vision was Flannery O'Connor, a young Catholic writer living in Georgia, who described the subject of all her stories as being "the action of grace on a character who is not very willing to support it." In her fiction O'Connor frequently depicted characters who were stopped short, stripped of their illusions—whether of bourgeois virtue, social status, smug rationalism, or quiet good taste—so that they might receive a deeper truth about their own sins and their need for forgiveness. Often, in writing to correspondents who doubted that Catholic faith could be reconciled with human intelligence, she recommended Teilhard's writings by way of rebuttal. But out of all of Teilhard's work it appears that the concept of passive diminishment struck a particularly personal chord.

Early in O'Connor's life she was diagnosed with lupus, the same degenerative disease that had killed her father. For her survival she depended on regular cortisone shots that gradually dissolved her joints and made it difficult to walk without crutches. Her condition confined her to her family's dairy farm outside Milledgeville, Georgia, where she wrote as her strength permitted—two hours in the morning—and otherwise tended the menagerie of ducks, swans, and peafowl with which she surrounded herself.

O'Connor possessed a sharp ear for the absurd and capacity to reconcile what she called the comic and the terrible. She disliked sentimental piety and reacted strongly against the temptation of critics to drag her medical history into a consideration of her work. Yet her illness imposed a discipline and sense of priorities that she managed to turn to the advantage of her art. In her letters she appropriated Teilhard's phrase "passive diminishment" to describe a quality she admired, the serene acceptance of whatever affliction or loss no effort was likely to change. "I have enough energy to write with," she said, "and as that is all I have any business doing anyhow, I can with one eye squinted take it all as blessing. What you have to measure out, you come to observe closer."

Although the Catholic framework of her writing was widely recognized, it was the posthumous publication of O'Connor's letters that best revealed her own character and the deep correspondence between her artistic "message" and her own spiritual voice. She believed that her highest responsibility as an artist was to the good of her art. But as a Christian she also regarded her own life as a work in progress. The meaning of such a life is not measured in outward success. Our highest responsibility as human beings—again, in Ignatius's phrase—is "to praise, reverence, and serve God," employing the relative gifts we possess in the circumstances that are given us. As O'Connor noted, "The creative action of the Christian's life is to prepare his death in Christ. It is continuous action in which this world's goods are utilized to the fullest, both positive gifts and what Père Teilhard de Chardin calls 'passive diminishments.'"

O'Connor died at age thirty-nine. Her short life was lacking in external drama ("Lives spent between the house and the chicken yard do not make exciting copy"). But while she was restricted in her mobility, it is hard to think that hers was an impoverished life. She was no mystic in the usual sense, yet she lived deeply from the standpoint of what she called the central Christian mystery, the same insight that Julian of Norwich received in her divine "showings": that this world has, "for all its horrors, been found by God to be worth dying for."

🌿 🌿 🌿

In *City of God,* St. Augustine provided a catalog of various types of suffering beginning with "the love of futile and harmful satisfactions, with its results: carping anxieties, agitations of mind, disappointments, fears, frenzied joys, quarrels, disputes, wars, treacheries, hatreds," and so forth. He went on to list "fears of disaster," not to mention all the dreaded calamities that have nonhuman sources ("and they are past counting"), including "the extremes of heat and cold; of storm, tempest, and flood. . . the terror of being crushed by falling buildings, of the bites of wild animals, sudden accidents. . . ." This inventory, which is hardly exhaustive, continues for several pages.

In fact, the thread of suffering runs so deeply through the fabric of our existence that were it pulled free, the remnant would unravel beyond recognition. We learn to walk by stumbling and falling. Our progress is curbed by dead ends and disappointments, which no one can entirely escape. Illness and pain, whether of body or mind, are unavoidable. If we are spared serious illness, it touches those who are closest to us, and we feel their anguish.

All these facts may seem obvious. Still, within the culture of affluence and "entitlement" it is possible to imagine that suffering is somehow extrinsic to human existence, an unfortunate accident that befalls other people. But such evasion takes us only so far.

Suffering is a fact. The important question is how we face it. As Thomas à Kempis wrote in *The Imitation of Christ*, "The cross always stands ready, and everywhere awaits you. You cannot escape it, wherever you flee; for wherever you go, you bear yourself, and always find yourself." He went on to pose these alternatives: "If you bear the cross willingly it will bear you and lead you to your desired goal, where pain shall be no more. . . . If you bear the cross unwillingly, you make it a burden and load yourself more heavily; but you must needs bear it. If you cast away one cross, you will certainly find another, and perhaps a heavier." In a sense those people who come through excruciating experiences not just whole but transformed represent a kind of miracle. We dare not feel at ease at any moment in some sense of reassurance that suffering is really "okay." Those who suffer demand compassion and practical solidarity, not glib solutions to the "problem" of suffering.

Yet we can repeat what the saints learned from experience. By identifying their suffering with the cross of Christ, they found more than consolation; they found a way to transfigure their suffering, binding themselves more intimately to the love of God and to more compassionate union with their neighbors. Here is perhaps the most troubling lesson the saints teach us, yet the most crucial, in our consideration of happiness. We have limited control over the circumstances of our lives. But we have the power in every circumstance to shape our attitudes. Thus, while we can be miserable in the midst of comfort and luxury, it is equally possible—as the saints are witnesses—to be happy in the midst of suffering.

The early church fathers liked to use the image of a mousetrap to describe how God, using Jesus as "bait," contrived to catch Satan. It is a homely image that somewhat dulls the shocking reality of death on a cross. But it resonates with the experience of those saints who, in their suffering, attempted to join themselves to the pattern of Christ. It can speak to us too in our suffering.

The trap has sprung. But we are not caught. The deepest part of ourselves is far away, in our true country, beyond the land of thunder, frost, and "falling buildings," at the still center of the turning world.

❦

24

Learning to Love: Notes in Solitude

John Daniel

I'm reminded, reading Thomas Merton, that I'm drawn to the language of Christianity. How can I not respond to those vast, resonant nouns—*name, word, love, spirit, father, son, hope, God, faith, light, darkness, peace?* To speak or write those words, even casually, is to stir depths I do not know. I'm also drawn to the activeness of Merton's Catholicism. Meditation for him—he calls it "inner silence"—"depends on a continual seeking, a continual crying in the night . . ."

I cried in the night once. When my mother was dying, on a respirator in intensive care, I was strung out with anguish and one night prayed for relief. I didn't know to whom or what I was praying. Later that night, while I slept, help came. I saw my mother as she had been the day before she fell and broke her hip, only now she seemed made of light—her cheerful face, her silvery hair, her lavender skirt and orange blouse, all was radiant. With the vision came the understanding that my mother couldn't live in her body anymore, yet she would live. When I woke into my thinking mind I didn't know *how* she would live, how she could, but the vision was the vision, and it helped.

Since then I've felt inclined to pray at times. But without an emergency pressing me, I've balked at the problem of to whom, to what? The idea of a God who can hear prayer, who knows individuals and responds to them personally, has always given me trouble. My reasoning mind resists. In fact, it seems to me that such a notion condemns the believer to neurosis or outright insanity, for how can it be squared with the facts of human and nonhuman violence and misery, the horrific deaths and torments that occur every day? How does a caring God countenance the murder of children, and how does a caring person countenance such a God?

And yet I cry in the night.

The feelings of my heart turn me toward the Spirit whose name I do not know. Whether it knows me I can't say, but at times I sense knowing all around me in this brimming silence. I sense it in the council of trees surrounding my meadow at dusk, in the swirl and slide of the green river. It's in the rank havens where bears even now are stirring toward wakefulness, in the flight of the owl and osprey, in the black-tailed deer and in the cougar that takes the deer down. It's the Spirit of beginnings and of ends, of necessity and of chance, of the one way and the many. Its name, though I do not know it, glitters in fire across the sky tonight, is spoken clearly by the whispering river, is as close as the ground I stand on and the breath that clouds and vanishes before my face. Death will loosen my grasp and darken my sight. All things are transient, from sow bugs to the stars. And only in their transience and our own, here, now, can we sometimes touch the eternal and taste its joy.

🍃

25

Eucharist and Solitary Confinement

Pedro Arrupe, SJ

I personally experienced a deep sense of pain for the lack of the Eucharist during the thirty-three days that I was imprisoned in Japan, but there was also at the same time a feeling of the faithful and consoling presence of Our Lord. The enemies of Christianity had made a thousand accusations against me. They were angry, since they saw that while they were trying to put obstacles in the way to conversions, a good number of young people were turning to the church and were receiving baptism. The war broke out in Japan on the feast of the Immaculate Conception, 1941, with the attack on Pearl Harbor.

The military police immediately put me in jail, in a cell with an area of four square meters. I did not know why they had put me there, and I was not told why for a long time, and only at the end of my confinement.

I passed the days and nights in the cold of December entirely alone and without a bed, or table, or anything else but a mat on which to sleep. I was tormented by my uncertainty on why I had been imprisoned. This provoked a kind of self-torture because of the presumptions, suspicions, and fears that I had done something that could have been a source of harm to others. But I was above all tortured by not being able to say mass, at not being able to receive the Eucharist. What loneliness there was! I then appreciated what the Eucharist means to a priest, to a Jesuit, for whom the mass and the tabernacle are the very center of his life. I saw myself dirty, unshaven, famished, and chilled to the bone without being able to talk with anyone. But I felt even more anguish for my Christians who were perhaps suffering because of me. And above all there was no mass. How much I learned then! I believe that it was the month in which I learned the most in all my life. Alone as I was, I learned the knowledge of silence, of loneliness, of harsh and severe poverty, the interior conversation with "the guest of the soul" who had never shown himself to be more "sweet" than then.

During those hours, those days, those weeks of silence and reflection I understood in a more illuminating and consoling way the words of Christ: "Remember what I have told you: a servant is not more important than his master. If they have persecuted me, they will also persecute you" (John 15:20). I was interrogated for thirty-six hours in a row. I was asked matters that were very touchy to answer, and I was myself astonished by the "wisdom" and the fitness of my replies. It was a proof of the saying of the Gospel: "Do not be concerned about what you must say to defend yourselves. I shall give you the right words and I shall give you such wisdom that all your adversaries will not be able to resist and much less defeat you" (Luke 21:14–15).

When my sufferings were becoming more cruel, I experienced a moment of great consolation. It was Christmas night. My mind went back to so many happy Christmases, to the three masses which I was able to celebrate that night. What remembrances filled my mind! But none of all this was now possible. I was alone, without mass. Instead of Christmas it seemed more like Good Friday! Just then when my Christmas was being changed into the passion and that blessed night into a sad Gethsemane, I heard a strange sound near one of the windows. It was the soft murmur of many voices which, with muted accents, sought to escape detection. I began to listen. If any of you have been in prison waiting for a sentence, you would appreciate the anxiety with which I followed those sounds which were now of themselves becoming an immediate source of suspicion. Such are the fears that one feels within the four walls where one is detained.

Suddenly, above the murmur that was reaching me, there arose a soft, sweet, consoling Christmas carol, one of the songs which I had myself taught to my Christians. I was unable to contain myself. I burst into tears. They were my Christians who, heedless of the danger of being themselves imprisoned, had come to console me, to console their

Shimpu Sarna (their priest), who was away that Christmas night which hitherto we had always celebrated with such great joy. What a contrast between that thoughtfulness and the injustice of senseless imprisonment!

The song with those accents and inflections which are not taught or learned poured forth from a touching kindness and sincere affection. It lasted for a few minutes; then there was silence again. They had gone and I was left to myself. But our spirits remained united at the altar on which soon after would descend Jesus. I felt that he also descended into my heart, and that night I made the best spiritual communion of all my life.

26

The Good That Rises When the Bottom Falls Out of Life

Joni Woelfel

Years ago, when I got home from being in the hospital, I was so weak I could barely walk. My husband set up a cot for me in our main floor office so I wouldn't have to navigate stairs. I was a young mother at the time and had never felt so helpless.

However, I was filled with the need for creativity, along with the desire to be able to control at least something! Needing to be surrounded by some of my sacred things, I decided to gather a small collection on our fireplace mantle by my bed, where I could be comforted by it. I crept around the house, practically on my hands and knees, but managed to set up photos of my kids, a scented votive candle, a small dried floral arrangement, a stack of my favorite books, a display of get-well cards and other meaningful objects.

When I was done, I felt a surge of joy despite the changes long-term illness was bringing. This was my initiation into understanding author Joseph Campbell's words: "We must be willing to let go of the life we planned so as to have the life that is waiting for us."

That reminds me of the time when our yard was besieged by black mold following months of torrential rains and humidity. Our plants, deck and even our plastic white lawn chairs were covered with the awful black stuff. We treated it repeatedly with bleach, cleansers and even re-painting, but the mold always relentlessly came back. We ended up chopping down our many perennials and stopped fighting that which couldn't be fought.

Author Julia Cameron wrote, "The creative process is a process of surrender, not control," and that was certainly the case that year. Gardening is a deeply soul-filling practice for me, as I am a lifelong farm kid whose well-being depends on digging in the dirt. Not being able to work outside as I looked out the window at the big mess caused me to spend wasted time on feeling anxious, uptight and frustrated. As poet Maya Angelou said, "You may not control all the events that happen to you, but you can decide not to be reduced by them."

We want to control suffering, the weather, the safety of our loved ones, our emotions, anger, what people think, stress, tragedy—the list goes on and on. We do not relish being vulnerable, feeling frightened, judged or needing help when this could be translated as weakness. We want to be empowered, which is the essence of life management, maturity, achieving goals and making a difference in the world. What happens then, when the bottom falls out of life in big and small ways and we face diminishment? Are we no longer in control or empowered?

The answer is that we learn a deeper kind of empowerment that doesn't depend on external conditions so much as on inner strength, faith, optimism and hope. Henri Nouwen wrote: "Hope is willing to leave unanswered questions unanswered and unknown futures unknown. Hope makes you see God's guiding hand."

When we see through the eyes of the soul, we learn that God's guidance and consolation through prayer, patience, a lot of adjusting and love empower us. When I look back at the timeline of my life, I can see that this is true on many levels. Indeed, I find I keep coming back to the words by Campbell: "The rapture that is associated with being alive is what it's all about."

For many of us, this is evidence of the divine presence always there, filling the spaces between control, surrender and letting go all our lives through.

Sparks

There is a crack in everything.
That's how the light gets in.

—LEONARD COHEN

You have to keep breaking your heart
until it opens.

—RUMI

In every human being there is a special
heaven, whole and unbroken.

—PARACELSUS

❦

27

Startled by Joy

Carlo Carretto

I'd gone off to Africa and joined the novitiate of the Little Brothers of Jesus at El Abiodh in Algeria. I went to the Little Brothers of Father de Foucauld in response to a call to consecration heard in my heart and requiring a clear answer from me. The idea of giving myself to the last and least of the earth, the poorest of the poor—the thought of merging myself in the dough of the world as living leaven—attracted me. I wanted to devote my existence to others and I wanted to do it where the going would be tough. The desert would be the perfect place, I thought. "Present to God, and present to people," was the way the great mystic of the Sahara Charles de Foucauld put it, and I wanted to embody those two tensions at unity in a life where contemplation and action went hand in hand. And there in the novitiate of the Little Brothers I began to dream, and dream, and dream.

Do you know what I dreamed about? I dreamed about becoming a Little Brother and living the gospel among men and women who had need of me and my witness. And who were these brothers and sisters of mine, in my dream? Whenever we think of "others" we have no choice but to limit the picture in our mind, and narrow it down to some particular group of people, depending on our experience, and especially depending on our feelings.

One of us will think of the Chinese and say, "I'll devote myself to the Chinese." Someone else thinks of the poor of the Third World with their starving babies, the peasants of Latin America, and decides, "I'll devote myself to them." One of my fellow novices told me he wanted to sneak into a country behind the Iron Curtain and devote himself to the victims of atheistic propaganda. Another one told me he would go to Hong Kong to work to build a Christianity that would be equal to face the problems of China when Hong Kong becomes part of China again.

Do you know what I wanted to do? I was dreaming too and plans were taking shape in my heart and mind. My dream was to go to the Alps and live with the Alpine rescue teams up on the Matterhorn and go with them to help people caught in storms.

Dreams don't happen by accident.

All my life I had been a mountain climber. I'd been captain of an Alpine team, and the mountains were my passion. I wanted to devote my passion to my fellow beings caught in the snow. I wanted to be brother to Alpine guides and devote to their work, which is certainly not easy, my prayers and my service, as Jesus inspired me. But I was only dreaming.

Do you know what happened to me in the middle of my dream? I had to go on a four-hundred-mile hike through the Khaloua desert from El Abiodh. I was not in very good condition and a male nurse, my friend, who took good care of me was concerned. "I'll give you some shots," he said. "You'll see, they'll keep you going."

"Fine," I said.

And with the best of intentions my friend stuck a needle in my thigh and injected me with a paralyzing poison. In less than twenty-four hours my leg was useless. He had made a mistake. He'd used the wrong vial.

It was stupid, but I would not say the nurse had been at fault except in the sense that he was impulsive and careless. I didn't complain then, and I tried to keep cheerful if only to help the nurse whose fault it was not to go out of his mind, he was not as emotionally stable as I was.

As soon as I felt a little better I started thinking things over. What about my dream now? What about the Alpine rescue team? Goodbye dream. Farewell any hope of ever climbing the Matterhorn. Suddenly I felt cheated. How could I have been betrayed in this way? I'd come to Africa to become a Little Brother. I'd wanted to devote myself to people dying in snowstorms, I wanted to save them. Had I been wrong to want that? What a perfectly miserable state of affairs! How could the God I wanted to serve not reach out his hand when I needed him? Why didn't he step in and stop such a simple, stupid mistake? Why didn't he help me? Why did he let. . . .

Sisters and brothers, let's stop for a moment. Let each of us think of our own suffering, our own trouble, our own paralysis, our own story. What am I doing here?

How did I get in this wheelchair? What am I doing with this crutch?

How come I can't sleep at night?

How did I ever marry such a man, and then he abandons me to boot?

Why did that beam have to fall on me in the earthquake and crush my arm?

Why am I alone?

What's wrong with just wanting to get married? And now there's no hope.

Why can't I draw just one easy breath of air?

Is someone else to blame for all this? Or worse, is it because I'm so disordered inside?

And then, why does God, this so-called God, permit things like this?

Why doesn't he step in in time?

Why did he just stand and watch while some idiot wretch beat me within an inch of my life and now I'll never be able to walk again?

Why didn't he make Herod die before he could carry out the slaughter in Bethlehem because Jesus was a thorn in his side?

Why didn't he step in and stop that storm blowing my hut away where I lived on the shore as a poor fisherman, as poor as Jesus himself?

Does this God exist or not?

Well, if he does, why doesn't he act, why doesn't he make an exception for me? Here I came to serve him, and all he seems to do is mock me and let me turn into a cripple. I thought it was a good idea to devote myself, as a mountaineer, to my fellow beings freezing to death in the snow! And now what? What am I to do now? Not join the Alpine rescue team, that's for sure! So He's really switched things on me! Or could it be up to me to change plans? Could be.

Thirty years have passed since then—thirty years since my dream went wrong. Now here I am in front of you, and you have your dreams too, or have had them. And I can tell you something. That mistaken injection that paralyzed my leg was not a stroke of bad luck. It was a grace. Let's be precise. There's no point in pious platitudes. It was bad luck, yes. It was a misfortune. But God turned it into a grace. I had a useless leg. I could not climb. So I got a Jeep and became a meteorologist. Through no wish of my own, there I was where I belonged: in the desert. Instead of trudging through the snow I trudged through the sand. Instead of mountain passes I came to know caravan routes. Instead of chamois I saw gazelles. Life suddenly appeared to me as it was, an immense personal exodus. Now I saw the desert as an extraordinary environment of silence and prayer. My crippled leg helped me to "stand firm" (James 1:12). I the runner—now stood firm. I who'd always tried to do two things at once—now stood firm. No doubt about it, it was a plus.

Deep down inside I began to understand that I hadn't been cheated. Misfortune had thrust me upon new paths. Brothers and sisters before me with your misfortunes, I testify to you of one thing only. Today, thirty years after the incident that paralyzed my leg, I don't say it wasn't a misfortune. I only say that God was able to transform it into a grace. I have experienced in my flesh what Augustine says: "God permits evil, so as to transform it into a greater good." God loves his children, and when he sees that someone or something has hurt them, what imagination he has—to transform the evil into good, inactivity into contemplation, the cry of pain into a prayer, grief into an act of love!

I know I'm only a child, telling you these things. Smart people don't tell you. They're embarrassed. Well, I'm going to come right out and tell you. I've found no other answer to my pain. And I know it by experience. You can be happy with a crippled leg. Very happy. In my experience the wounds of poverty and suffering produce a special, very precious, very sweet honey. It's the honey of the Beatitudes proclaimed by Jesus in the Sermon on the Mount. I have tasted this honey and have become convinced of the rationality of the gospel, of the reasons for so many mysterious things. I have been convinced by experience. I have come to believe in God through experience, and I always say: I believe in God because I know him. And from suffering too.

There is still plenty of room for mystery. And it is right that this should be so, to educate us in humility, which is so important in our relationship with the Absolute that is God. But I the thickest cloak that weighed on my misery and my blindness God has torn away, and the nakedness of my wounded flesh has helped me to recognize, out beyond the veil of mystery, the nakedness of God. Only then, startled by joy, did I know the truth, that the encounter with the Eternal is possible. And that it is stupendous.

〰

28

Transforming the
Heart of Suffering

Pema Chödrön

In order to have compassion for others, we have to have compassion for ourselves. In particular, to care about other people who are fearful, angry, jealous, overpowered by addictions of all kinds, arrogant, proud, miserly, selfish, mean—you name it—to have compassion and to care for these people, means not to run from the pain of finding these things in ourselves. In fact, one's whole attitude toward pain can change. Instead of fending it off and hiding from it, one could open one's heart and allow oneself to feel that pain, feel it as something that will soften and purify us and make us far more loving and kind.

The tonglen practice is a method for connecting with suffering—ours and that which is all around us—everywhere we go. It is a method for overcoming fear of suffering and for dissolving the tightness of our heart. Primarily it is a method for awakening the compassion that is inherent in all of us, no matter how cruel or cold we might seem to be.

We begin the practice by taking on the suffering of a person we know to be hurting and whom we wish to help. For instance, if you know of a child who is being hurt, you breathe in the wish to take away all the pain and fear of that child. Then, as you breathe out, you send the child happiness, joy, or whatever would relieve their pain. This is the core of the practice: breathing in other's pain so they can be well and have more space to relax and open, and breathing out, sending them relaxation or whatever you feel would bring them relief and happiness. However, we often cannot do this practice because we come face to face with our own fear, our own resistance, anger, or whatever our personal pain or our personal stuckness happens to be at that moment.

At that point you can change the focus and begin to do tonglen for what you are feeling and for millions of others just like you who at that very moment are feeling the same stuckness and misery. Maybe you are able to name your pain. You recognize it clearly as terror or revulsion or anger or wanting to get revenge. So you breathe in for all the people who are caught with that same emotion and you send out relief or whatever opens up the space for yourself and all those countless others. Maybe you can't name what you're feeling. But you can feel it—a tightness in the stomach, a heavy darkness, or whatever. Just contact what you are feeling and breathe in, take it in—for all of us and send out relief to all of us.

People often say that this practice goes against the grain of how we usually hold ourselves together. Truthfully, this practice does go against the grain of wanting things on our own terms, of wanting it to work out for ourselves no matter what happens to the others. The practice dissolves the armor of self-protection we've tried so hard to create around ourselves. In Buddhist language one would say that it dissolves the fixation and clinging of ego.

Tonglen reverses the usual logic of avoiding suffering and seeking pleasure and, in the process, we become liberated from a very ancient prison of selfishness. We begin to feel love both for ourselves and others and also we begin to take care of ourselves and others. It awakens our compassion and it also introduces us to a far larger view of reality. It introduces us to the unlimited spaciousness that Buddhists call shunyata. By doing the practice, we begin to connect with the open dimension of our being. At first we experience this as things not being such a big deal or as solid as they seemed before.

Tonglen can be done for those who are ill, those who are dying or have just died, or for those who are in pain of any kind. It can be done either as a formal meditation practice or right on the spot at any time. For example, if you are out walking and you see someone in pain—right on the spot you can begin to breathe in their pain and send out some relief. Or, more likely, you might see someone in pain and look away because it brings up your fear or anger; it brings up your resistance and confusion. So on the spot you can do tonglen for all the people who are just like you, for everyone who wishes to be compassionate but instead is afraid, for everyone who wishes to be brave but instead is a coward.

Rather than beating yourself up, use your own stuckness as a stepping stone to understanding what people are up against all over the world. Breathe in for all of us and breathe out for all of us. Use what seems like poison as medicine. Use your personal suffering as the path to compassion for all beings.

꧁

29

The Empty Cage

Kate Chopin

There was once an animal born into this world, and opening his eyes upon Life, he saw above and about him confining walls, and before him were bars of iron through which came air and light from without; this animal was born in a cage.

Here he grew, and throve in strength and beauty under the care of an invisible protecting hand. Hungering, food was ever at hand. When he thirsted water was brought, and when he felt the need to rest, there was provided a bed of straw upon which to lie; and here he found it good, licking his handsome flanks, to bask in the sun beam that he thought existed but to lighten his home.

Awaking one day from his slothful rest, lo! the door of his cage stood open: accident had opened it. In the corner he crouched, wondering and fearingly. Then slowly did he approach the door, dreading the unaccustomed, and would have closed it, but for such a task his limbs were purposeless. So out the opening he thrust his head, to see the canopy of the sky grow broader, and the world waxing wider.

Back to his corner but not to rest, for the spell of the Unknown was over him, and again and again he goes to the open door, seeing each time more Light.

Then one time standing in the flood of it; a deep indrawn breath—a bracing of strong limbs, and with a bound he was gone.

On he rushes, in his mad flight, heedless that he is wounding and tearing his sleek sides—seeing, smelling, touching of all things; even stopping to put his lips to the noxious pool, thinking it may be sweet.

Hungering there is no food but such as he must seek and ofttimes fight for; and his limbs are weighted before he reaches the water that is good to his thirsting throat.

So does he live, seeking, finding, joying and suffering. The door which accident had opened is opened still, but the cage remains forever empty!

〰️

30

The Meaning of Suffering

Pierre Teilhard de Chardin, SJ

Human suffering, the sum total of suffering poured out at each moment over the whole earth, is like an immeasurable ocean. But what makes up this immensity? Is it blackness, emptiness, barren wastes? No, indeed: it is potential energy. Suffering holds hidden within it, in extreme intensity, the ascensional force of the world.

The whole point is to set this force free by making it conscious of what it signifies and of what it is capable. For if all the sick people in the world were simultaneously to turn their sufferings into a single shared longing for the speedy completion of the kingdom of God through the organizing of the earth, what a vast leap toward God the world would thereby make!

Sparks

*No man is an island, entire of itself;
every man is a piece of the continent, a
part of the main . . . any man's death
diminishes me, because I am involved
in mankind. . . .*

—JOHN DONNE

*If one part of the body suffers, every
part suffers with it. If one part is honored, every part rejoices with it.*

—1 CORINTHIANS 12:26

*We are already one. But we imagine
that we are not. And what we have to
recognize is our original unity. What we
are to be is what we are.*

—THOMAS MERTON

PART THREE

FROM LIGHT, LOVE

Love one another as I have loved you.

—JESUS

31

Jerusalem

Naomi Shihab Nye

"Let's be the same wound if we must bleed.
Let's fight side by side, even if the enemy
is ourselves: I am yours, you are mine."
—TOMMY OLOFSSON, SWEDEN

I'm not interested in
who suffered the most.
I'm interested in
people getting over it.

Once when my father was a boy
a stone hit him on the head.
Hair would never grow there.
Our fingers found the tender spot
and its riddle: the boy who has fallen
stands up. A bucket of pears

in his mother's doorway welcomes him
        home.
The pears are not crying.
Later his friend who threw the stone
says he was aiming at a bird.
And my father starts growing wings.

Each carries a tender spot:
something our lives forgot to give us.
A man builds a house and says,
 "I am native now."
A woman speaks to a tree in place
of her son. And olives come.
A child's poem says,
 "I don't like wars,
they end up with monuments."
He's painting a bird with wings
wide enough to cover two roofs at
        once.

Why are we so monumentally slow?
Soldiers stalk a pharmacy:
big guns, little pills.
If you tilt your head just slightly
it's ridiculous.

There's a place in my brain
where hate won't grow.
I touch its riddle: wind, and seeds.

144

Naomi Shihab Nye

Something pokes us as we sleep.

It's late but everything comes next.

32

When Hope and History Rhyme

Seamus Heaney

Human beings suffer,
They torture one another,
They get hurt and get hard.
No poem or play or song
Can fully right a wrong
Inflicted and endured.

The innocent in gaols
Beat on their bars together.
A hunger-striker's father
Stands in the graveyard dumb.
The police widow in veils
Faints at the funeral home.

History says, don't hope
On this side of the grave.

Seamus Heaney

But then, once in a lifetime
The longed-for tidal wave
Of justice can rise up,
And hope and history rhyme.

So hope for a great sea-change
On the far side of revenge.
Believe that further shore
Is reachable from here.
Believe in miracle
And cures and healing wells.

Call miracle self-healing:
The utter, self-revealing
Double-take of feeling.
If there's fire on the mountain
Or lightning and storm
And a god speaks from the sky

That means someone is hearing
The outcry and the birth-cry
Of new life at its term.

❧

33

We Do Whatever We Can

Jon Mundy

What do we do when we see someone who is suffering? We do whatever we can. We talk on the phone with them; we give them some of our time; we help with some project or maybe some money.

> What do we live for if not to make life
> less difficult for other people.
> —GEORGE ELIOT (1819–1880)

I like to keep a few bills in the pocket of the car door to give to folks who make a living out on the streets. One hot summer day, as I pulled into a parking spot at a large mall, I saw a middle-aged woman with a withered arm limping toward my car. She looked pretty beaten up and shuffled along as though she had suffered a stroke. I knew she was going to be asking for some money, so I got a few bills ready for her. She said she needed $7 for the day and then she could get a room for the night.

As I handed her the money, suddenly a woman in a white Mercedes pulled up beside the two of us, rolled down her window, and yelled out: "She is always out here you know!" "Yes," I said, "This is her job. We are obviously taken care of. It is a hard way to make a living, walking around all day in a hot parking lot asking for help." With that the woman in the Mercedes hit her accelerator, and she was gone. The woman with the withered arm looked at me and said: "Thank you for understanding." We were both richer for that moment.

🍃

34

Your Heart Will Be Broken, and Yet . . .

Henri J. M. Nouwen

Do not hesitate to love and to love deeply.

You might be afraid of the pain that deep love can cause. When those you love deeply reject you, leave you, or die, your heart will be broken. But that should not hold you back from loving deeply. The pain that comes from deep love makes your love ever more fruitful. It is like a plow that breaks the ground to allow the seed to take root and grow into a strong plant. Every time you experience the pain of rejection, absence, or death, you are faced with a choice. You can become bitter and decide not to love again, or you can stand straight in your pain and let the soil on which you stand become richer and more able to give life to new seeds.

The more you have loved and have allowed yourself to suffer because of your love, the more you will be able to let your heart grow wider and deeper. When your love is truly giving and receiving, those whom you love will not leave your heart even when they depart from you. They will become part of yourself and thus gradually build a community within you.

Those you have deeply loved become part of you. The longer you live, there will always be more people to be loved by you and to become part of your inner community. The wider your inner community becomes, the more easily you will recognize your own brothers and sisters in the strangers around you. Those who are alive within you will recognize those who are alive around you. The wider the community of your heart, the wider the community around you. Thus the pain of rejection, absence, and death can become fruitful. Yes, as you love deeply the ground of your heart will be broken more and more, but you will rejoice in the abundance of the fruit it will bear.

Sparks

*Compassion—which means, literally,
"to suffer with"—is the way to the
truth that we are most ourselves, not
when we differ from others, but when
we are the same. Indeed the main spiritual question is not, "What difference
do you make?" but "What do you have
in common?" It is not "excelling" but
"serving" that makes us most human.
It is not proving ourselves to be better
than others but confessing to be just like
others that is the way to healing and
reconciliation.*

—Henri J. M. Nouwen, *Here and Now*

*There is a Father who weeps with us;
there is a Father who sheds tears of
infinite compassion for his children.
We have a Father who knows how*

to weep, who weeps with us. A Father
who awaits us in order to console us,
because he knows our suffering and has
prepared a different future for us. This
is the great vision of Christian hope,
which expands over all the days of our
life, and seeks to raise us up once more.

—POPE FRANCIS,
"GENERAL AUDIENCE,"
AUGUST 23, 2017

That which is hateful to you, do not do
to another. That is the whole Law. The
rest is commentary. Now go and learn.

—RABBI HILLEL

🕯

35

Compassion Is Stronger than Loathing

Joyce Rupp

Suffering has saturated my life for a long time—not so much my own afflictions, although there have been enough of those. The suffering I know best belongs to others: A beloved spouse dying in surgery. Lung cancer. Life-threatening motorcycle accident. Piercing divorce. Longings for a child never birthed. Unjust imprisonment. Alzheimer's at a way-too-early age. Physical and sexual abuse. Metal rods under the thin skin of a body that never stops hurting. PTSD revealed in the tears of an elderly war veteran. Malicious infidelity. You name the suffering and it has probably entered my heart's domain through the life of someone else.

I have learned much about compassion because of the visitation of other people's suffering. Being a companion to sorrow, hurt and travail has taught me about the mysterious soul of humanity, its wide landscape of resilience, and the depths of faithful love. I thought I was at home with suffering, but I wasn't ready for the source coming unexpectedly from a man I had never met.

One day a letter arrived from "Daniel" who was incarcerated a few states away. This kind of mail was not unusual. Sometimes prisoners find my name from books or articles on spirituality available for them to read. I've corresponded with a variety of inmates over the years, grateful to lighten the load of their loneliness and add a bit of positive connectedness with someone "on the outside."

For two years the letters went back and forth between Daniel and me. As time passed, I noticed the content of his letters sounded more "churchy." I wondered, "Is he a religious leader? Maybe an ordained clergyman?" I never ask personal questions in my letters, nor about the type of crime that led to the prisoner's conviction. I didn't ask this time, either.

Then the month came when my envelope to Daniel returned with the memo: "no longer at this address." I thought he might have been released, but three months later he wrote to tell me he had been transferred. For some uncanny reason, I looked at the name of the new correctional facility on the return address and thought, "I could go online and find out what kind of crime this man committed." Two minutes later, I was looking at the face of a person whose crime was listed as "statutory sodomy and child molestation," two counts each.

I sat staring at that data and felt sickened. Here was the last type of prisoner I wanted to engage with in any sort of correspondence or remote relationship. Everything in me wished I had not searched for the information. The bilious thought of thousands of maimed children, ruthlessly damaged due to pedophiles—including the actions of Daniel—was almost too much to consider. I closed the file, deeply disturbed by the decision I knew lay ahead: would I continue the correspondence? Could I bear that sort of suffering to invade my life? I was extremely unsure. Continuing to relate to someone who had caused such immense harm seemed impossible.

Prayer. Journaling. Confidential conversations with a close friend, then with a spiritual director. Back and forth the emotions and thoughts churned inside of myself. The question of "yes or no" would not leave me alone: "Can I sustain correspondence with this person? No, I can't do it. I would never accept the actions of a pedophile. Everyone who violates another human being, especially an innocent child, ought to be imprisoned for the crime and be accountable for it." But then another view would come forth: "Yes, I can continue writing to him. I cannot turn away from this person who suffers from an addiction that will affect him the rest of his life. Doesn't Jesus say everyone deserves forgiveness? Doesn't each person, no matter how vile their actions, deserve a second chance? Maybe my continued support will help Daniel find strength and courage to never act out of that abhorrent behavior again."

The more I reflected on pedophilia, the more I returned to the gospel where Jesus reaches out to touch the leprous man, the one rejected by society and forced out of the circle of humanity. If there is any group today treated like the lepers of Jesus' era, it is undoubtedly that of pedophiles. Disgust, hatred, loathing—these are typical emotional responses of the public who despise those who sexually assault children. I know, because I have been one of those "public."

I have slowly been able to envision Daniel's suffering as not only involving external imprisonment but internal imprisonment, as well. What might his interior suffering be like? If he is able to empathize with the terrible consequences of his victims, is it devastating for him to live with that reality? Does he loathe himself or find any worth in who he is? What does he see for his future?

I hold onto the hope that Daniel can learn how to control and manage his sexual addiction, just as those in recovery from drug and alcohol abuse have learned to do. The results of research by the U.S. Justice Department show that recidivism rates for sex offenses are lower than for all other major types of crimes. This fact strengthens my hope for his rehabilitation.

My repulsive response continues to lessen the more I envision Daniel as a suffering human being. I continue to write to him because I have prayerfully reached inside my heart and found compassion to be stronger than loathing. I can now say, "Yes, this suffering, too, can enter into the circle of my life."

❧

36

Bald Places:
Notes on Nursing as Witness

Hob Osterlund

Rooms 652 and 653 couldn't be more different, except they're both bald.

Room 652 is a woman with a glioblastoma. It's the kind of brain tumor that often kills fast, usually within six months of diagnosis. She's 57. Her name is Teea. The doctor says I'm history, says Teea softly, without apparent fear. Her humor is deceptive. I bet she'd bribe, threaten, or supplicate all creatures, medical or otherwise, two-legged or four, who promised they could buy her even one extra week. She wants to live so bad she could scream it to the heavenly rafters, but she doesn't, at least not in the hospital. She behaves calmly here.

Each of her three daughters is as beautiful as their mama, even though radiation therapy fried the hair right off their mama's head. She only has curly clumps above her ears now, like a clown. I'm thinking of having them bronzed, she says, so she can put the last follicular evidence from the upper end of her body on her mantle above the fireplace, next to her baby boots. Nobody remarks that the boots are from the beginning of her life and the hair is likely to be from the end of it.

The oldest daughter is studying primates somewhere in Africa, and came home two days after her grandmother telephoned. The middle daughter's in the air force, is training to be a pilot. The youngest lives nearby, her dancer's body temporarily compromised by an unexpected pregnancy offered as a good-bye gift from a yoga instructor. All three are with their mother in the hospital as regular as rain.

Teea figures the lion's share of her own parenting duties are behind her, and she wants to sit back on some padded chaise lounge, drink a nice Australian wine, and watch her daughters do what they do best. She wants to be the audience. Applaud, witness, detach if she can, but not die.

Room 653 is bald too, clean-shaven after smashing into a windshield of a stolen car he careened into oncoming traffic. Both the men he hit died right there on the highway—a father driving his visiting son to the airport, a young and popular volleyball player, finishing his college career with 731 digs. His grinning picture was all over the news.

Even though the wreck was mid-afternoon, 653's blood toxicology screen was positive for methamphetamines, benzodiazepines, alcohol, and cocaine.

He's skinny. Street drugs suppressed his appetite's voice, tricking him into thinking he was not just high, but full. At first glance his body looks like it belongs to an emaciated, dying old man. Closer up it's easy to see his sculpted muscles are like hardwood. He's seventeen years old. He wears a plastic diaper, and his limbs are splayed like a book, his feet and hands tied to each corner of the bed so he doesn't hurt himself or us nurses. He yells nearly constantly. Most of the noises are unintelligible, but he does seem to know three words: *sit, no, how.* We're suspicious that sit is a mispronunciation. More often than not, how is a long sound with several syllables, like a chant. The emphasis is usually on the ow, leading us to wonder if he's in pain. We nurses give him analgesics even though the meds don't seem to do much. We give the meds because it makes us feel like we're doing something useful. We give them because his yelling drives us crazy.

He's a hard one to like, is 653. Most of the time all we can do is re-tie him, put mitts on his hands so he doesn't chew into his own fingers or scratch himself bloody, clean him up from time to time. I've never seen anyone visit him, but there's a note on his board that says *Grandma and Noni love you. Get well soon.*

For someone tethered in four places, 653 is all over the bed. In just two weeks he's already rubbed his heels down to the bone. His diaper hangs low on his angled hips, and most of the time he's able to squirm out of it. If he gets his hands loose he tears up the diaper and eats it. Or throws punches. Last week he gave a night shift nurse a nasty bruise on her upper arm while she was pushing a syringe of liquid food into a gastric tube going into his abdomen. While her focus was on his G-tube, he bit through the wrist restraint and swung at an enemy none of the rest of us can see.

Teea is my age, and we've had a few good talks about God and destiny and health. Today, however, I spend my precious few extra moments here with 653. I don't really want to, but my job (as a pain and palliative care clinical nurse specialist) is to assess his discomfort. I also want to relieve the pain of the staff nurses, which will happen briefly if I can quiet him down.

His name is Brandon. I discovered yesterday that if I call him by name, he stops yelling. But when I start to leave he just starts up again, no matter how many tranquilizers or opiates the nurses give him.

"Brandon!" I shout over his shout. He makes full-on eye contact and stares like a baby does, not quite in focus but very intent on something he sees. Does he recognize his own name long enough to stop the spinning of some kaleidoscope of fears that dominate his visual field?

"Brandon, do you have pain?"

"No," he says, as clearly as if we'd just resumed a lucid conversation over a cup of coffee.

I take a couple of charts into his room. After I say his name and he goes silent, I do some paperwork. He stares at me, he stares at the walls, he stares into thin air. Every once in a while he tracks something across the ceiling, as if a shooting star has flared above him. His temporary quiet is a relief.

I tell him about things. Tonight I tell him I want to make a movie of him, to show high school kids what really happens on drugs. I figure the diaper might get them. I ask him how could it be that some people want to live with every fiber of their spirit, and others seem to dare death to come get them. Brandon doesn't argue or interrupt. He lies there in total silence. He doesn't do it because he hears just any words, but because he hears a voice speak his name. His name is his talisman, his clue, his Geiger counter, his compass, his home base, his organizer, his horizon, his divining rod.

"Brandon, I have to go." He stares at my lips as if he hears something remotely familiar and unnerving, like the pulsing of a troubled mother's heart.

Heading toward Teea's room, I see her husband, Robbie, leaning against the wall outside her door. His eyes greet me with a grief as dense as the door itself, and a question that has no answer. Still, his grief is soft somehow, a metal tempered with gratitude. Grief tempered by guilt is barbed wire.

I lean up against the wall next to him. He tells me that the hardest thing about Teea's diagnosis is the helplessness. A high school biology teacher, he likes tangibles. He tells me the ground beneath his feet moves like sand, he cannot find purchase.

Noooooooooooooo, shouts Brandon from 653.

I follow Robbie into Teea's room.

Honey, says Teea, seeing her husband's helplessness. *Go sit with that young man next door*, and Robbie leaves willingly, taking his question with him.

37

I Thought I Was There to Help a Son and His Dying Father—Then This Happened

Rabbi Steve Leder

"Rabbi, do you make house calls?" the man named Mackie on the other end of the phone wanted to know. "My dad was never religious but he said he'd like to see a rabbi before he dies. He's living with us now. He has no place else to go and he can't get out any more. It's cancer. Please?"

The address was up a winding, urban Los Angeles canyon—traffic whizzing by, houses packed up against each other like so many kernels on an ear of corn. The front yard was brown and weedy with a broken sprinkler and a folding chair off to the side. I knocked and Mackie let me in.

"Dad, the rabbi is here to talk to you," Mackie said loudly over his shoulder. "Go ahead, rabbi. He's in the living room on the couch."

Mackie looked much older than when I last saw him. I'd officiated at his wedding some five years before. Now, he was gray and balding. He was tired. When I found his father Bert on the couch I knew why.

Bert was in the last stages of lung cancer, his skin thin, spotted and brittle as a dead leaf. His body was mostly bones and his face so gaunt his eyes seemed too large for his head. I sat next to him, yet a universe away, in my navy suit, crisp white shirt, polished shoes and dimpled tie.

Bert, in his diaper, gray sweat pants and undershirt with a leak-proof pad beneath him, looked at me. He had no idea who I was or why I was there. Although he wasn't in pain, every gesture, every syllable, took more strength than he had to spare.

I wanted to help Bert. So in my most compassionate rabbi's voice, I said, "Bert, I'm the rabbi. I know you wanted to see me? How can I help?"

Bert slowly rotated his head in my direction, locked in on me with his huge, brown eyes and whispered, "I have to take a crap."

I said I was here to help, I thought to myself, but there's a limit. You want to talk theology, you want to pray, you want to plan your funeral with me—I'm game. You want me to change your diaper—I'm out. I went to find Mackie.

"Uh, I think he has to go to the bathroom," I said timidly. Mackie sighed and headed toward the living room. I pulled back to watch a remarkable dance unfold.

"Okay Dad," Mackie said facing his father on the couch and bending over. "Put your arm around my neck. Come on Dad. Put it up there. That's right. Come on. Now the other one. Don't let go Dad."

With Mackie's help, Bert managed to put both of his stick-like arms around Mackey's neck and lace his fingers together.

"On three Dad. One, two, three—up we go. That's it. Don't let go," Mackie urged Bert as he slowly lifted him off the couch so that they were now face to face. Bert's body slumped against Mackie's. His arms still locked in place behind Mackie's neck. Mackie's arms were around Bert's waist. Then, the dance began—the most tender dance I have ever seen.

"That's it Dad," Mackie encouraged, as he slowly rocked from side to side while Bert shuffled an inch or two forward with movement, all the time Mackie with all his strength. Ever so gently, Mackie maneuvered them both towards the bedroom where Bert could lie down and have his diaper changed.

"That's it. Good Dad. Now I know why mom said you were such a great dancer." Side to side. Inch by inch. The old man and his middle-aged son, holding on to each other against the sadness and the ache—swaying to a melody only they could hear.

Bert died a week later. When I met with Mackie to learn more about his dad before the funeral I found out why Bert was living with him. Bert was broke. His first wife had thrown him out for losing all their money on scams. His second wife threw him out for the same reason. That's when Bert moved in with Mackie.

Bert had a joke for every occasion. He was down and out so often that he had a special place in his heart for anyone in trouble. He couldn't do a favor for you fast enough once you asked him. He was a snappy dresser, loved elephants, could fly a plane and man, could he dance. And Bert could sell anything.

In the 70s he was the guy who showed up on your doorstep to sell you a vibrating bed. Just give him a second to set up the demo model in your living room. In the 80s it was shoes. In the 90s oil well investments. Bert always knew that wealth and power were just around the corner and all he had to do was mortgage the house to get there.

When Bert was dying, Mackie was all he had. Mackie was his only child. They shared the same birthday. They shared the same apartment 50 years ago and now the same house. When Mackie was a boy Bert used to come home late from work some nights, wake Mackie up, bounce him in his bed and toss him in the air.

Then, "One, two, three—up we go," on to the kitchen counter, feeling 10-feet tall, to dip graham crackers in cold milk. Sometimes, Bert gave Mackie a bath. In the end, Mackie had to clean up Bert's messes. There was a beautiful, fearful symmetry to it all. Bert's wives left him. His friends turned out to be crooks. His son's wife wanted Bert in a home. But Mackie just hung in there with his dad, gathering up the fragments of a life that once was, and placing them in the holiest of places—his heart.

So it is with fathers and sons who love each other come what may: "One, two, three," and "Up we go," dancing to a melody only we can hear.

❦

38

I Am Your Brother

Bob McCahill, MM

> *Where I am, there also will my servant be.*
>
> —JOHN 12:26

One evening I returned home by bus, having admitted a few children to Dhaka hospitals. Rain was falling as I began my walk to the hut in the dark. Within minutes I felt a sharp bite on my foot. I flashed my light and saw a snake slithering away.

You could say I was worried. Over 6,000 people die from snakebites each year in Bangladesh.

So I decided to call on my neighbor. When Alom realized the danger, he started to pray out loud, applying pressure to my foot. Then Kobad arrived on the scene and applied pressure, too, starting at my head and working down to the snakebite. In the morning Alom came to check on me. "Still living," I assured him. "By the grace of the Almighty," he declared.

Worrying over snakebites isn't the only thing that will disturb your sleep in Bangladesh. For all its beauty, it is a country continually struggling for survival. Almost 156 million people—about half the size of Iowa. Close to half of them live in poverty, and children are malnourished. Many have birth defects. With personal income about $1.25 a day, you can see the consequences of poverty without trying hard.

For more than 30 years, my mission here has been simple: I live the way Jesus did, caring for the poor. I take children to the hospital for evaluations and surgeries. I visit the homebound to make sure they are taking their medicines and do not feel alone. I write letters for women who find certain conversations too difficult to have with their doctors. I help patients with paperwork they don't understand. The wonderful thing about my mission is that once someone knows what I do, they tell a neighbor. A farmer ran from his rice field one day to stop me as I was passing by, obviously aware of my work. He said a child needed surgery, and inquired if I could help.

I explained that I am a Christian missionary. "If you are a Christian," he asked, "why would you help a Muslim?" I told him that as long as we are serving one another, we are serving God.

I was able to reinforce this point one day at a tea stall where men gather for serious conversation. Janhangir and his friends wanted to know more about my faith. So I told them. After listening, Janhangir said how fortunate he felt to know why I live among them—because of the life and teachings of Jesus.

Sparks

My heart sickens at all the sadness in
     the sweet,
the sweetness in the sad.

—FRANCIS THOMPSON

There comes a moment to everyone
When Beauty stands staring into the
     soul
With sad sweet eyes
That sicken at the sound of words.
And God help those who pass that mo-
     ment by.

—EDMOND ROSTAND, *CYRANO DE BERGERAC*

❦

39

The Bread of Life

Miriam Therese Winter, MMS

Another day. Another long, hot, hard, exhausting, exasperating day in Ethiopia. Well, better one day in Your tent, O God, O suffering, saving, compassionate God, than a thousand in the security of my own home in Connecticut. It is time to celebrate the "liturgy" for which I was ordained. I pull on my jeans and my thick-soled shoes. God, I believe, help my unbelief. God, let all that I do praise you.

It is just after dawn and already the long, brown, deathly silent line snakes all around the perimeter of our camp and loses itself in the distance. Our intense feeding center for emaciated children is a temporary refuge. Daily, every two hours, what serves as bread is figuratively blessed, broken, and distributed under a variety of disguises: soybean porridge or hotcake; high protein biscuits; thick, sweet powdered milk laced with oil and sugar; and once in a while, God be praised, a very, very small banana.

Seven times a day I take, break, bless, distribute, and all around give thanks as the Author of life restores to life those physically diminished. Seven times a day, a miracle, when fully present to the Presence, I can see the shape of grace. It is 10 a.m., time once again for me to fulfill my primary daily function, presiding over a "liturgy of the Eucharist," presiding over the distribution of desperately needed "daily bread." When you see a hungry person and feed that person, you are feeding me, said Jesus. I look out over the beautiful brown faces of my sisters and brothers, broken bodies with unbroken spirits. This is my body, said Jesus. Amen, I say. Amen.

40

Ingrown Toenails and the Body of Christ

Adele Gonzalez

A few years ago I hiked the White Mountains of New Hampshire with my family. What I had not shared with anyone was that for weeks I had been suffering from an ingrown toenail in my big toe. After a couple of hours my toe was throbbing. I could hardly walk and was slowing down the group. The children were getting frustrated. Finally, my brother stopped and said, "Sit on that rock and give me your boot."

In shock I watched him cut off the entire top part of my boot with his hunting knife. "Here," he said, "the toe won't bother you anymore. It has all the space it needs now to move freely without hurting." I cannot describe my relief and that of the rest of the family. My brother didn't heal my toe, but he gave it the space it needed to stop affecting the entire body.

This true story touched a truth in me that has lasted a long time: The suffering of one member of the body affects the entire body. In the words of St. Paul: "If one part suffers, all the parts suffer with it" (1 Corinthians 12:26). Because of a simple pain in my big toe, my whole being felt sick. The physical pain did not touch my family; however, the consequences of my discomfort were ruining their hiking trip.

That day I realized again the interconnectedness of all creation. My soul saw things that went beyond what my senses were revealing to me: What happened to the people that had to look for an alternate trail because we had obstructed ours for more than 20 minutes, not to mention the beauty we were missing because of the delay? Could there be a commonality between my toe, my family, humanity and even creation?

In times of intimacy with God, I often reflect on the "ingrown toenails" that appear in my life in the most ordinary ways. There was a mentally challenged child who once spent the entire Sunday Mass making loud noises. I could hardly believe some of the parishioners' comments: "They shouldn't bring people in that condition to church. I've been distracted and angry for the whole Mass. Couldn't that family sit in the crying room?" On another occasion a divorced lady who had recently remarried went with her husband to receive Communion. A group complained to the priest because he had allowed this mortal sin to be committed before his own eyes. Maybe they expected an announcement in the parish bulletin about the canonical status of the woman's previous marriage.

The sense of hopelessness transmitted by the media makes me wonder if the grudge that I am holding against a very good friend because of something that happened a long time ago has anything in common with the hatred among some tribes in the Middle East. The conflict between Israel and Palestine is acted out in many households today. Brother against brother, families against families, engaging in mean controversies over the right to inherit the land of their parents. We also continue to damage the Earth with the cars we drive, the pesticides we use to grow our produce, and the chemicals applied to preserve our meats, among other things.

Questions crowd my mind as I think again about my ingrown toenail. What do we do with those who cause pain to the body of Christ? Do we try to heal them and make them comfortable? Do we give them some space so they don't hurt so much? Or do we complain, ignore and try to get rid of them?

It never occurred to any member of my family, regardless of their annoyance, to send me back to the hotel. In spite of their frustration, I did not feel rejected or unwanted. Nobody suggested that I should have taken care of my problem before our vacation. I was their sister, aunt, sister-in-law, friend whom they loved who just happened to have a problem.

In the body of Christ, which transcends buildings and denominations, we are often blind and fail to recognize the person, the beloved son or daughter of God, and Mother Earth, which we continue to dominate. With our narrow vision we see only a "retarded child," a "sinful woman" or an opportunity to make more money no matter what. What does God expect of us?

Jesus spent his life revealing a God who tore down walls, who welcomed all and became vulnerable to all. Jesus revealed God's unconditional hospitality to all. In a very concrete way, my ingrown toenail taught me to respect and have compassion for every member in the body of Christ.

"If one member of the body suffers, all suffer together with it; if one member is honored, all rejoice together with it."

41

The Cup of Sorrow
Is Also the Cup of Joy

Henri J. M. Nouwen

When I first came to l'Arche Daybreak, I saw much sorrow.

I was asked to care for Adam, a twenty-two-year-old man who could not speak, could not walk alone, did not show signs of recognition. He had a curved back, suffered from daily epileptic seizures, and often had intestinal pains. When I first met Adam, I was afraid of him. His many handicaps made him a stranger to me, a man I wanted to avoid.

Soon after I met Adam I also came to know his brother Michael. Although Michael could speak a little and was able to walk by himself and even fulfill some minor tasks, he too was severely handicapped and needed constant attention to make it through the day. Adam and Michael are the only children of Jeanne and Rex.

Michael lived at home until he was twenty-five and Adam until he was eighteen. Jeanne and Rex would have loved to continue to keep the boys at home. However, time was eroding the physical resources required to look after their sons and so they entrusted them to the l'Arche Daybreak community hoping to find a good home for them there.

I was quite overwhelmed with the sorrows of this little family. Four people burdened by worries and pain, by fear of unexpected complications, by the inability to communicate clearly, by a sense of great responsibility, and by an awareness that life will only become harder as age increases.

But Adam, Michael, and their parents are part of a much greater sorrow. There is Bill, who suffers from muscular dystrophy, who needs a pacemaker for his heart and a breathing machine for his lungs during the night, and who is in constant fear of falling. He has no parents to visit. His parents never were able to care for him, and both died at a rather young age.

There is Tracy, completely paralyzed, but with a bright mind, always struggling to find ways to express her feelings and thoughts. There is Susanne, not only mentally disabled but also regularly battered by inner voices that she cannot control. There is Loretta, whose disability causes her to feel unwanted by family and friends and whose search for affection and affirmation throws her into moments of deep despair and depression. There are David, Francis, Patrick, Janice, Carol, Gordie, George, Patsy . . . each of them with a cup full of sorrow.

Surrounding them are men and women of different ages, from different countries and religions, trying to assist these wounded people. But they soon discover that those they care for reveal to them their own less visible but no less real sorrows: sorrows about broken families, sexual un-fulfillment, spiritual alienation, career doubts, and most of all, confusing relationships. The more they look at their own often wounded pasts and confront their uncertain futures, the more they see how much sorrow there is in their lives.

And for me things are not very different. After ten years of living with people with mental disabilities and their assistants, I have become deeply aware of my own sorrow-filled heart. There was a time when I said: "Next year I will finally have it together," or "When I grow more mature these moments of inner darkness will go," or "Age will diminish my emotional needs." But now I know that my sorrows are mine and will not leave me. In fact I know they are very old and very deep sorrows, and that no amount of positive thinking or optimism will make them less. The adolescent struggle to find someone to love me is still there; unfulfilled needs for affirmation as a young adult remain alive in me. The deaths of my mother and many family members and friends during my later years cause me continual grief. Beyond all that, I experience deep sorrow that I have not become who I wanted to be, and that the God to whom I have prayed so much has not given me what I have most desired.

But what is our sorrow in a little community in Canada, compared with the sorrow of the city, the country and the world? What about the sorrow of the homeless people asking for money on the streets of Toronto, what about the young men and women dying of AIDS, what about the thousands who live in prisons, mental hospitals, and nursing homes? What about the broken families, the unemployed, and the countless disabled men and women who have no safe place such as Daybreak?

And when I look beyond the boundaries of my own city and country, the picture of sorrow becomes even more frightening. I see parentless children roaming the streets of São Paulo like packs of wolves. I see young boys and girls being sold as prostitutes in Bangkok. I see the emaciated prisoners of war in the camps of former Yugoslavia. I see the naked bodies of people in Ethiopia and Somalia wandering aimlessly in the eroded desert. I see millions of lonely, starving faces all over the world, and large piles of the dead bodies of people killed in cruel wars and ethnic conflicts. Whose cup is this? It is our cup, the cup of human suffering. For each of us our sorrows are deeply personal. For all of us our sorrows, too, are universal.

Now I look at the man of sorrows. He hangs on a cross with outstretched arms. It is Jesus, condemned by Pontius Pilate, crucified by Roman soldiers, and ridiculed by Jews and Gentiles alike. But it is also us, the whole human race, people of all times and all places, uprooted from the earth as a spectacle of agony for the entire universe to watch. "When I am lifted up from the earth," Jesus said, "I shall draw all people to myself" (John 12:32). Jesus, the man of sorrows, and we, the people of sorrow, hang there between heaven and earth, crying out, "God, our God, why have you forsaken us?"

"Can you drink the cup that I am going to drink?" Jesus asked his friends. They answered yes, but had no idea what he was talking about. Jesus' cup is the cup of sorrow, not just his own sorrow but the sorrow of the whole human race. It is a cup full of physical, mental, and spiritual anguish. It is the cup of starvation, torture, loneliness, rejection, abandonment, and immense anguish. It is the cup full of bitterness. Who wants to drink it? It is the cup that Isaiah calls "the cup of God's wrath. The chalice, the stupefying cup, you have drained to the dregs" (Isaiah 5 1:17) and what the second angel in the Book of Revelation calls "the wine of retribution" (Revelation 14:8), which Babylon gave the whole world to drink.

When the moment to drink that cup came for Jesus, he said: "My soul is sorrowful to the point of death" (Matthew 26:38). His agony was so intense that "his sweat fell to the ground like great drops of blood" (Luke 22:44). His close friends James and John, whom he had asked if they could drink the cup that he was going to drink, were there with him but fast asleep, unable to stay awake with him in his sorrow. In his immense loneliness, he fell on his face and cried out: "My Father, if it is possible, let this cup pass me by" (Matthew 26:39). Jesus couldn't face it. Too much pain to hold, too much suffering to embrace, too much agony to live through. He didn't feel he could drink that cup filled to the brim with sorrows.

Why then could he still say yes? I can't fully answer that question, except to say that beyond all the abandonment experienced in body and mind Jesus still had a spiritual bond with the one he called Abba. He possessed a trust beyond betrayal, a surrender beyond despair, a love beyond all fears. This intimacy beyond all human intimacies made it possible for Jesus to allow the request to let the cup pass him by become a prayer directed to the one who had called him "My Beloved." Notwithstanding his anguish, that bond of love had not been broken. It couldn't be felt in the body nor thought through in the mind. But it was there, beyond all feelings and thoughts and it maintained the communion underneath all disruptions. It was that spiritual sinew, that intimate communion with his Father, that made him hold on to the cup and pray: "My Father, let it be as you, not I, would have it" (Matthew 26:39).

Jesus didn't throw the cup away in despair. No, he kept it in his hands, willing to drink it to the dregs. This was not a show of willpower, staunch determination, or great heroism. This was a deep spiritual yes to Abba, the lover of his wounded heart.

When I contemplate my own sorrow-filled heart, when I think of my little community of people with mental handicaps and their assistants, when I see the poor of Toronto, and the immense anguish of men, women, and children far and wide on our planet, then I wonder where the great yes has to come from. In my own heart and the hearts of my fellow people, I hear the loud cry, "O God, if it is possible, let this cup of sorrow pass us by." I hear it in the voice of the young man with AIDS begging for food on Yonge Street, in the little cries of starving children, in the screams of tortured prisoners, in the angry shouts of those who protest against nuclear proliferation and the destruction of the planet's ecological balance, and in the endless pleas for justice and peace all over the world. It is a prayer rising up to God not as incense but as a wild flame.

From where then will come that great yes? "Let it be as you, not I, will have it." Who can say yes when the voice of love hasn't been heard! Who can say yes when there is no Abba to speak to? Who can say yes when there is no moment of consolation?

In the midst of Jesus' anguished prayer asking his Father to take his cup of sorrow away, there was one moment of consolation. Only the Evangelist Luke mentions it. He says: "Then an angel appeared to him, coming from heaven to give him strength" (Luke 22:43).

In the midst of the sorrows is consolation, in the midst of the darkness is light, in the midst of the despair is hope, in the midst of Babylon is a glimpse of Jerusalem, and in the midst of the army of demons is the consoling angel. The cup of sorrow, inconceivable as it seems, is also the cup of joy. Only when we discover this in our own life can we consider drinking it.

❧

42

The End of Suffering

Joseph F. Girzone

It has become overwhelmingly clear as I recount memories of the past and all the stories I have listened to that suffering is the lot of human beings on this earth. I know of no one who has escaped it. As my friend Mike Leach says, "No one gets out of this thing alive."

Every day we see on television tragedies from natural disasters and cataclysmic occurrences worldwide, where often hundreds of thousands of lives are destroyed, or permanently damaged. From all this it is easy to see that suffering and pain is universal. What is so difficult for us to understand is our inability to find a reason for such suffering. All we can say is that it is a frightening phenomenon testifying to a sick and dysfunctional world society. As impossible as it is for us to understand the meaning of all this suffering, it is still critical that we learn to accept the fact of its existence and learn to deal with it in a way that will prevent it from destroying us or crippling us in the living out of our own lives, lives that we must learn to live not just for ourselves but in a way that we can make our own contribution, great or small, to alleviate the suffering of our brothers and sisters around the world, suffering which could be reduced if more people cared enough to do something.

Fortunately, we have the examples of so many strong and heroic souls who have, by their wisdom, endurance, and limitless patience, taught us ways to understand pain and suffering and, by their example, showed us the way to rise above even the most horrifying personal tragedies and fashion a life for themselves that is not only personally productive but further inspiration to others who are struggling with similar seemingly insurmountable suffering. Many of these people through their own suffering have reached out to heal others. What is their source of strength?

Rarely does it come from human sources, because from a purely natural point of view suffering is of little value in situations that seem hopeless or purposeless. From practically all the heroic, suffering persons I have met, their strength comes from an intimacy with God, that in many instances manifests a strange mystical experience that helps them rise above their pain and find joy in their experience of closeness to God, or an intangible presence in their lives that they cannot define, but they know and have the strong conviction that they are not suffering alone. For those with faith they draw strength from knowing that God is with them, and they often feel that their suffering bonds those of them who are Christians to the crucified

Jesus with whom they feel that their own suffering helps to save straying souls.

There are so many beautiful persons who have risen above their own personal traumas and each year spend weeks and months traveling to faraway places to help rebuild the lives of the hopeless and destitute. There is a parish in Burke, Virginia, whose pastor had suggested to his parishioners that they give up a meal a week during Lent and donate the money saved to help the poor. This parish has a large number of federal government workers as well as people in the military. The first Lent the parish embarked on this program they collected $60,000. With that money a group of parishioners with their pastor went to Haiti and with the help of the people there built a number of houses for the poor. It has now been eight years since the parish embarked on this dream, and they decided to make it a full-time project. They have collected close to $2,000,000 and have built thousands of homes, and a school and other buildings necessary to better the life of the community there. The wonderful thing about this group is that they don't think they are doing anything sensational; they are just thrilled to be able provide a better existence for a destitute people struggling to stay alive.

They are Good Shepherds who harken, sooner or later but surely, the end of suffering. They inspire us not to wallow in the inevitability of suffering but to enter it and, by entering it, transform it.

Sparks

Early one morning on the steps of Precious Blood Church, a woman with cancer on the face was begging (beggars are allowed only in the slums) and when I gave her money (no sacrifice on my part but merely passing on alms which someone had given me) she tried to kiss my hand. The only thing I could do was kiss her dirty old face with the gaping hole in it where an eye and a nose had been. It sounds like a heroic deed but it was not. One gets used to ugliness so quickly. What we avert our eyes from one day is easily borne the next when we have learned a little more about love. Nurses know that, and so do mothers.

—Dorothy Day

*Love is the measure by which we will
be judged.*

—Dorothy Day, *After John of the Cross*

We are all meant to be mothers of God.

—Meister Eckhart

43

Prayer of Loving Kindness

May I be filled with loving kindness.
May I be well.
May I be filled with loving kindness.
May I be well.
May I be peaceful and at ease.
May I be whole.

May you be filled with loving kindness.
May you be well.
May you be filled with loving kindness.
May you be well.
May you be peaceful and at ease.
May you be whole.

May we be filled with loving kindness.
May we be well.
May we be filled with loving kindness.
May we be well.
May we be peaceful and at ease.
May we be whole.

Sources and Acknowledgments

Orbis Books has made every effort to identify the owner of each selection in this book, and to obtain permission from the author, publisher, or agent in question. In the event of inadvertent errors, please notify us.

1. Therese J. Borchard, "A Beginning." From *Beyond Blue: Surviving Depression & Anxiety and Making the Most of Bad Genes* (New York: Center Street Books, 2009).

2. James Martin, SJ, "Why Is There Suffering?" Excerpt of 1,380 words [as appeared in Huffington Post 3/14/11: "Why Is There Suffering"] from *The Jesuit Guide to (Almost) Everything: A Spirituality for Real Life* by James Martin, SJ. Copyright © 2010 by James Martin, S.J. Reprinted by permission of HarperCollins Publishers.

3. Maryanne J. Kane, "I Don't Have an Explanation, and Yet . . ." Originally titled "Why Does a Loving God Permit Pain?" From *National Catholic Reporter*, Soul Seeing, February 21, 2017. https://www.ncronline.org.

4. Victor M. Parachin, "Changing Our Relationship to Pain." From *Eastern Wisdom for Western Minds* (Maryknoll, NY: Orbis Books, 2007), 134–37.

5. Michael Leach, "It's Okay to Despair and Swear at God." From *National Catholic Reporter*, Soul Seeing, May 20, 2014. https://www.ncronline.org.

6. Pico Iyer, "The Value of Suffering," from the *New York Times* © 2013 The New York Times Company. All Rights reserved. Used under license.

7. Patrick T. Reardon, "I Found God in the Pain of My Brother's Suicide." From *National Catholic Reporter*, Soul Seeing, forthcoming. https://ww.ncronline.org.

8. Tom Smith, "We Don't Take Her Breath for Granted." From *National Catholic Reporter*, Soul Seeing, October 4, 2016. https://www.ncronline.org.

9. Steve Duin, "I Hold His Hand." From *Father Time* (Portland, OR: Arnica), originally published in *The Oregonian,* November 24, 1994.

10. Bruce Lawrie, "Who Am I, Lord, That You Should Know My Name?" From Brian Doyle, *A Sense of Wonder* (Maryknoll, NY: Orbis Books, 2016), 150–52, originally published in *Portland Magazine.*

11. Dorothee Soelle, "God on the Gallows." From *Suffering*, trans. Everett Kalin of *Leiden,* 1973. Copyright © 1975, 1984 by Fortress Press. Reprinted by permission of Fortress Press. All rights reserved.

12. Patrick Giles, "When I Knew: Godlessness and God on September 11." From Brian Doyle, *A Sense of Wonder* (Maryknoll, NY: Orbis Books, 2016), 93–95, originally published in *Portland Magazine.*

13. Kate Bowler, "What I Really Want." From *Everything Happens for a Reason: And Other Lies I've Loved* by Kate Bowler, copyright © 2018 by Kate Bowler. Used by permission of Random House, an imprint and division of Penguin Random House LLC, and SPCK, London. All rights reserved.

14. David J. Unger, "I Thought I Knew Him: The Suffering Humanity of Christ." From *Commonweal Magazine*, March 22, 2019. Copyright © Commonweal Foundation, reprinted with permission. For more information, visit www.commonwealmagazine.org.

15. Heidi Russell, "Love Leads to Suffering, but We Take the Risk to Love Because We Must." From *National Catholic Reporter*, Soul Seeing, January 8, 2019. https://www.ncronline.org.

16. Thich Nhat Hanh, "Why We Shouldn't Be Afraid of Suffering." Excerpt of 525 words [as appeared in *Tricycle,* June 28, 2017] from *The Art of Living* by Thich Nhat Hanh. Copyright © 2017 by Unified Buddhist Church, Inc. Reprinted by permission of HarperCollins Publishers.

17. Marianne Williamson, "The Search for God Is a Search for Light." Excerpt from pp. xi–xii from *Tears to Triumph* by Marianne Williamson. Copyright © 2016 by Marianne Williamson. Reprinted by permission of HarperCollins Publishers.

18. Ellen Bass, "The Thing Is." From *Mules of Love*. Copyright © 2002 by Ellen Bass. Reprinted with the permission of the Permissions Company, LLC, on behalf of BOA Editions Ltd. www.boaeditions.org.

19. Marianne Williamson, "Miracles Happen," originally titled "Surrendering Our Sorrow." Excerpt from pp. 1–3 from *Tears to Triumph* by Marianne Williamson. Copyright © 2016 by Marianne Williamson. Reprinted by permission of HarperCollins Publishers.

20. Richard Rohr, OFM, "There's Something Deeper Happening Here," originally titled "Transforming Pain." Posted in Daily Meditations at https://cac.org on October 17, 2018. Adapted from Richard Rohr, *A Spring within Us: A Book of Daily Meditations* (CAC Publishing, 2016), 199, 120–21. Reprinted by permission of CAC Publishing.

21. Stephen Colbert, "It's a Gift to Exist." Extracts from a CNN interview with Anderson Cooper broadcast on August 15, 2019.

22. Eckert Tolle, "Spiritual Awakening and Intense Suffering." Adapted from an interview with Tami Simon entitled "The Power of Now and the End of Suffering," https://www.eckharttollenow.com/article/The-Power-Of-Now-Spirituality-And-The-End-Of-Suffering. Copyright © 2019 Eckhart Teachings Inc. All rights reserved.

23. Robert Ellsberg, "Learning to Suffer." Adapted from *The Saints' Guide to Happiness: Practical Lessons in the Life of the Spirit* (New York: North Point Press, 2003). Reprinted by permission of Farrar, Straus & Giroux.

24. John Daniel, "Learning to Love: Notes in Solitude." Adapted from *Rogue River Journal: A Winter Alone* (Counterpoint Press, 2005).

25. Pedro Arrupe, SJ, "Eucharist and Solitary Confinement," originally titled "Eucharist and Youth." From *Other Apostolates Today* (Institute of Jesuit Sources, 1981), 296–300. Used with permission: © Jesuit Sources, Institute for Advanced Jesuit Studies, Boston College, Chestnut Hill, MA. All rights reserved.

26. Joni Woelfel, "The Good That Rises When the Bottom Falls Out of Life." From *National Catholic Reporter*, Soul Seeing, November 14, 2017. https://www.ncronline.org.

27. Carlo Carretto, "Startled by Joy," originally titled "Dreams Lost and Found." From *Why O Lord? The Inner Meaning of Suffering* (Maryknoll, NY: Orbis Books, 1986).

28. Pema Chödrön, "Transforming the Heart of Suffering." From Lion's Roar, January 11, 2018, https://www.lionsroar. com/transforming-the-heart-of-suffering/. Originally appeared in *Buddhadharma: The Practitioner's Quarterly* (Summer 2010). Reprinted with permission.

29. Kate Chopin, "The Empty Cage." From *The Awakening* (Chicago & New York: Herbert S. Stone, 1899).

30. Pierre Teilhard de Chardin, SJ, "The Meaning of Suffering," originally titled "The Meaning and Constructive Value of Suffering." From Neville Braybrooke, ed., *Teilhard de Chardin: Pilgrim of the Future* (New York: Seabury Press, 1964), 23–26.

31. Naomi Shihab Nye, "Jerusalem." From *Red Suitcase.* Copyright © 1994 by Naomi Shihab Nye. Reprinted with the permission of the Permissions Company, LLC, on behalf of BOA Editions, Ltd., www.boaeditions.org.

32. Seamus Heaney, "When Hope and History Rhyme." From *The Cure at Troy: A Version of Sophocles' Philoctetes* by Seamus Heaney. Copyright © 1990 by Seamus Heaney. Reprinted by permission of Farrar, Straus and Giroux, LLC and Faber and Faber Ltd.

33. Jon Mundy, "We Do Whatever We Can." Original contribution from Jon Mundy for *The Way of Suffering.*

34. Henri J. M. Nouwen, "Your Heart Will Be Broken, and Yet . . ." Originally titled "Love Deeply." From *The Inner Voice of*

Sources and Acknowledgments

Love: A Journey through Anguish to Freedom by Henri Nouwen, copyright © 1996 by Henri Nouwen. Used by permission of Doubleday, an imprint of the Knopf Doubleday Publishing Group, a division of Penguin Random House LLC. All rights reserved.

35. Joyce Rupp, "Compassion Is Stronger than Loathing." Original contribution from Joyce Rupp for *The Way of Suffering*.

36. Hob Osterlund, "Bald Places: Notes on Nursing as Witness." Published in *Portland Magazine*, Winter 2007, and in *A Sense of Wonder*, edited by Brian Doyle (Maryknoll, NY: Orbis Books, 2016), 98–101. Reprinted by permission of Hob Osterlund.

37. Rabbi Steve Leder, "I Thought I Was There to Help a Son and His Dying Father—Then This Happened." Excerpt adapted from *More Beautiful than Before; How Suffering Transforms Us*, by Steve Leder (Carlsbad, CA: Hay House, 2017).

38. Bob McCahill, MM. "I Am Your Brother." From *Dialogue of Life: A Christian among Allah's Poor* by Bob McCahill (Maryknoll, NY: Orbis Books, 1996).

39. Miriam Therese Winter, MMS. "The Bread of Life." From *The Singer and the Song: An Autobiography of the Spirit* (Maryknoll, NY: Orbis Books, 1999).

40. Adele Gonzalez, "Ingrown Toenails and the Body of Christ." From *National Catholic Reporter*, Soul Seeing, December 6, 2011, https://www.ncronline.org.

41. Henri J. M. Nouwen, "The Cup of Sorrow Is Also the Cup of Joy," originally titled "Cup of Sorrow." From *Can You Drink the Cup?* by Henri J. M. Nouwen. Copyright © 1996, 2006 by Ave Maria Press®, Inc., P.O. Box 428, Notre Dame, IN 46556, www.avemariapress.com. Used with permission of the publisher. For more information on Henri Nouwen please go to the Henri Nouwen Legacy Trust website at www.henrinouwen.org.

42. Joseph F. Girzone, "The End of Suffering." From *The End of Suffering* (Maryknoll, NY: Orbis Books, 2013), 119–24.

43. "Prayer of Loving Kindness," adapted from Traditional Buddhist Meditation.

INDEX OF CONTRIBUTORS

Pedro Arrupe, SJ (d. 1991) was superior general of the Society of Jesus from 1965 to 1983 and was instrumental in promoting a new mission for the Jesuits in terms of "the faith that does justice." **25**

Ellen Bass is coauthor of the bestselling *The Courage to Heal: A Guide for Women Survivors of Child Sexual Abuse*. She has also published several volumes of poetry, including *The Human Line*. **18**

Therese J. Borchard is a mental health writer and advocate. She is the founder of the online depression communities Project Hope & Beyond and Group Beyond Blue, and is the author of *Beyond Blue: Surviving Depression & Anxiety and Making the Most of Bad Genes* and *The Pocket Therapist*. **1**

Kate Bowler is an assistant professor at Duke Divinity School. A graduate of Yale Divinity School and Duke University, Bowler is the author of *Blessed: A History of the American Prosperity Gospel* and *Everything Happens for a Reason (And Other Lies I've Loved)*. **13**

Carlo Carretto (d. 1988) was a member of the Little Brothers of Jesus, the religious order inspired by the spirituality of Charles de Foucauld. He was author of more than a dozen books, including the best-selling *Letters from the Desert*. **27**

Index of Contributors

Index of Contributors

Other books in the Way Series from Orbis . . .

THE WAY OF GRATITUDE
READINGS FOR A JOYFUL LIFE

A hundred famous writers share their experiences, essays, fiction, poems, meditations, and inspired ideas on the joy of being thankful. These honest and heartfelt writings will add gladness to your days.

Contributors include Wendell Berry, J. K. Rowling, David Brooks, Joan Chittister, James Martin, Thich Nhat Hanh, Henri Nouwen, Mary Oliver, Richard Rohr, Joyce Rupp, David Steindl-Rast, Rowan Williams, and many others whose spiritual perceptions bring joy and faith to millions.

Michael Leach is publisher emeritus of Orbis Books and the author and editor of many books, including *Soul Seeing*.
James T. Keane is senior editor at *America* magazine.
Doris Goodnough is permissions coordinator for Orbis Books.

240 pp., paperback
ISBN 978-1-62698-232-1

ORBIS BOOKS
Maryknoll, New York 10545

From your bookseller or direct: OrbisBooks.com
Call toll free 1-800-258-5838 M-F 8-4 ET

THE WAY OF KINDNESS
Readings for a Graceful Life

A collection of essays, fiction, poems, meditations, and inspired ideas on the grace and rewards of being kind.

Contributors include Anne Lamott, Frederick Buechner, James Martin, Jack Kerouac, Mother Teresa, Dorothy Day, Jack Kornfield, George Saunders, Joan Chittister, Joyce Rupp, Richard Rohr, Henri Nouwen, Steve Hartman, and many others whose insights and spiritual perceptions bring compassion and grace to many.

Michael Leach is publisher emeritus of Orbis Books and the author and editor of many books, including *Soul Seeing*.
James T. Keane is senior editor at *America* magazine.
Doris Goodnough is permissions coordinator for Orbis Books.

256 pp., paperback
ISBN 978-1-62698-275-8

ORBIS BOOKS
Maryknoll, New York 10545

From your bookseller or direct: OrbisBooks.com
Call toll free 1-800-258-5838 M-F 8-4 ET

THE WAY OF FORGIVENESS
READINGS FOR A PEACEFUL LIFE

The third in the popular Orbis series, this poignant collection of inspiring true stories will foster healing and harmony for those seeking peace in their lives.

Includes writings of C. S. Lewis, Henri Nouwen, Dorothy Day, Harold Kushner, Richard Rohr, James Martin, Jack Kornfield, Anne Lamott, Mary Oliver, Frederick Buechner, and many others.

Michael Leach is publisher emeritus of Orbis Books and the author and editor of many books, including *Soul Seeing*.
James T. Keane is senior editor at *America* magazine.
Doris Goodnough is permissions coordinator for Orbis Books.

256 pp., paperback
ISBN 978-1-62698-322-9

ORBIS BOOKS
Maryknoll, New York 10545

From your bookseller or direct: OrbisBooks.com
Call toll free 1-800-258-5838 M-F 8-4 ET